# Hope in the Urban Schools

## Love Stories

# Hope in the Urban Schools:

## Love Stories

By

Cara Churchich-Riggs

Strategic Book Publishing and Rights Co.

Strategic Book Publishing and Rights Co.
12620 FM 1960, Suite A4-507
Houston TX 77065
www.sbpra.com

ISBN: 978-1-61897-722-9

# DEDICATION

I dedicate this book to the love of my life, my beautiful daughter, Shelby Riggs. You and I have been a team who loves and supports each other through rough times and celebrations. I am so proud of you for the young lady you are becoming, living your life with full gusto, and experiencing life and people with purposeful attention. I love that you are kind to everyone you meet and you always see the good in people without judgment. I love, too, that you have joined me on this journey at Omaha South High Magnet School, and you love it as much as I do. I know it is probably not easy all of the time, being the principal's daughter, but you have taken on that burden with such grace and maturity. I thank you for your support of your mom, who has worked hard to finally make the dream of completing this book a reality. You have been a great listener along the way, laughing and crying with me as each chapter was completed. You are my most important champion, as I am yours. I cherish the gift of being your mom.

# FOREWORD

One of the great satisfactions in an educator's professional life is to see one of his students pursue a teaching career. In my office hangs a picture of the last Senior High Student Senate I sponsored as a high school counselor before assuming various Central Office administrative positions. Among the young people pictured in that memorable high school leadership class is Cara Churchich, an enthusiastic, confident, and accomplished student who is now, Ms. Cara Riggs, Principal of South High Magnet School, in the Omaha Public Schools, Omaha, Nebraska. It has been a privilege to watch her grow personally and professionally.

Built on a foundation of support from a loving family, nurtured through dedication to conscientious study, hard work, and varied experience, and fostered by a sensitivity and advocacy for the welfare of others, Cara Riggs has achieved success as a teacher and an educational leader. She is and has always been a cheerleader for others, both literally and figuratively. The stories told in this book reflect an insight and love for the young people who go beyond their academic lives and hours in school. This author sees vulnerable teenagers, their goodness and the possibilities for success in life, a potential that cannot be measured by a standardized test, a grade on a report card or statistic in a school performance report.

Cara Riggs has dedicated her life to helping young people and has demonstrated the care and concern for them and their families throughout her career. Her generous, selfless quality was quite evident during her tenure as a middle school principal. Tragically, one of her students was abducted after getting off a bus and was found murdered several months later. During this time, Ms. Riggs created a caring community group that brought together the student's family, peers, and teachers. She was able to keep the family and classmates hopeful and focused during the time of not knowing what happened to the child. At the same time, she demonstrated remarkable leadership at school and in the community, as a rock of support and a guide for all concerned while they dealt with the tragedy.

Knowing preadolescent and adolescent youngsters and relating to them have been strong attributes of Cara Riggs and have served her well as a school leader. She has developed programs, such as one for teen parents, which provide the opportunities for students to complete their high school studies and graduate in spite of their out-of-school responsibilities. Her welcoming nature and genuine interest in young people are reflected in the increased enrollment at her school and in the high academic and social achievements of the students she serves.

This book is more than a compilation of true stories of experiences of one administrator in an urban public school in America. It is a mirror reflecting the human side of education, as experienced by Cara and all school administrators and teachers while they live out their daily commitment to the education of young people. The stories reflect the possibilities and opportunities for youngsters provided by educators in urban school districts in every state. These are teachers and administrators who see beyond the facades of bravado, the barriers of fear and insecurity, and the effects of poverty and racism. These are professionals who recognize the potential to be discovered and nurtured in the students they serve.

Dr. John Mackiel
Superintendent
Omaha Public Schools

# ENDORSEMENTS

Hope In The Urban Schools: Love Stories will give the reader a peek into the real school life of teenagers in the urban setting who—in spite of the challenges they face—are given hope by teachers and administrators who care and who will do more beyond the presentation of subject matter or normal classroom routines to ensure their success. If you are a teacher in any setting, you will be buoyed up as the stories recall your own experiences where you have given hope for the future to individual students and made a lifelong positive impact on a young person's life.

"I am grateful to Cara Riggs for sharing her experiences and the real life stories of students she has served. Her fire of enthusiasm, the confidence, the can–do, positive spirit, and genuine love for helping others started during her high school years continues to blaze and give light and hope to the next generation. As a reader, you will be challenged to think about youth in a new light and to appreciate the work of the urban public school educator in a new way. In these love stories, you will discover the wonderful hope available for students in the urban schools."

John Mackiel, Superintendent,
Omaha Public Schools

"Finally! An honest and raw look into the power of adult to student relationships in providing hope for our kids in challenging situations—what a breath of fresh air! At a critical time in our educational climate, Principal Cara Riggs has provided a loving insight into the complexities of creating public school atmospheres where *hope* can indeed conquer *hopelessness*. Cara has wittingly revealed a front row seat to the *real* issues of education, and those doubting whether the American system of education is lost will be encouraged by her stories. A "must read" for *anyone* who really cares about the education of our kids, and what's working. Bravo, Cara!"

Wes Hall, Author, Teacher Trainer,
National Keynote Speaker

"In the midst of an educational system that instructs teachers to 'teach to the test,' it is refreshing to read the true stories of Cara Riggs and the students of South High School. Similar to the struggles that the Freedom Writers and I faced, Riggs overcomes the stereotypes placed on the Omaha Public School system by making her campus a safe haven and an inspiring place to learn. "Hope in the Urban School: Love Stories" serves as an uplifting and poignant read and can enlighten educators on how to empower their own students to achieve greatness. Her story is a triumphant example of what can happen when a principal refuses to give up on the 'unteachable' kids."

Erin Gruwell, Freedom Writer's Foundation

"At a time when our country seems to be abandoning our public schools, this book is a 'must read' for anyone who claims to genuinely care about the future of our kids. The 'love stories' told through the voice of Omaha High School principal Cara Riggs, reflect the real-life stories of students facing the challenges in our country's schools, directly associated with poverty and what miracles can happen when we provide love, care, and access. This book truly provides evidence of *hope* and that there are strong school communities reinventing powerful places where students indeed succeed."

Susie Buffett, Sherwood Foundation ®

# CONTENTS

# INTRODUCTION

With the current backdrop of public education painting a picture of total despair, now is the perfect time to follow through with decades of a dream to write a book about the experiences I have had in my career. It was time to share, in my voice, the truth about the challenges that our students face in their lives, and how their personal situations affect their ability to believe in their own successes. It was time to reveal that inside our schools are kids tackling extraordinary issues and still finding success. I believe that their stories, with minimal editorials from me, are enough for readers to understand our kids.

With twenty-eight years in education, the stories are plentiful. Every day is a new script of dramatic content that illustrates the real life scenarios that our students wake up to and how the very special people in our schools reach out to them.

This book is not only a tribute to our kids, but my sincere attempt to reach out to the larger public and to diminish their relentless, unfair judgment of the young people across this country. It is my attempt, as well, to allow readers to get a front row seat into the realities of those same students, hoping those same readers will open their hearts and see hope and promise in our youth and then speak with hope about them.

The stories in this book also reveal a true picture of the great number of dedicated and passionate teachers that work with students across this country. My students represent many others like them. The teachers in our school also reflect the true picture of just how many are in the profession for all of the right reasons, mostly because they truly care about our kids. Most teachers teach with their hearts, not with pedagogy. Those are the people who achieve real success with their students. I believe—without exception—that absent of heart and passion and the ability to connect to kids positively, student achievement does not happen. The ability to connect with kids is the foundation of their success.

For future teachers anxious to begin this amazing career, I hope these stories validate the power they have in changing the paths of the young people in their classrooms. To teach kids and not just content is an enormous responsibility and takes commitment beyond what anyone can imagine until they experience it. Teaching is not for the weak, and resiliency is a prerequisite, without a doubt. But the rewards are never ending. To hear from a young person that you have changed their life is worth all of the sweat and tears that one puts into loving these kids. Watching them overcome adversity brings us back the next day and the next school year. To all of you, I wish you joy in your journey to inspire and provide *hope*.

# Chapter 1

## AMBER MARIE HARRIS—ANGEL OFF THE BUS

"There is no tragedy greater than the loss of a child." Dwight Eisenhower

"Weren't you the principal of Amber Harris?" I'm often asked. "What must that incident have been like to go through?" That is a loaded question from someone who wants to hear the story beyond what the media reported. I possess the private details of the saga that played out beyond the journalist's pen or the reporter's microphone or camera. The way in which I rewind the story in my mind reflects a look beyond the chronological sequence of publicly told facts. My lenses allow the recall to forever be both a curse and a blessing to have been this little girl's principal during that time. I'm glad they ask the question, "What was it really like?"

The truth is, never in my wildest nightmares could I have imagined the story of Amber Harris being played out in my real world the way in which it did. You see, middle school girls are supposed to come to school, have a thirteen–year-old's stories of silly fun and on-and-off-again friends, worry about the flavor of their newest lip gloss, wonder what it's like to kiss Bobby Johnson and stress over whether or not they've studied hard enough for their algebra test. They are supposed to get that fluffy feeling in their stomach when a boy tells his friend to find out if she'll be his girl and go out with him (whatever that means when neither of them is old enough to drive). They are supposed to be able to sneak the forbidden pair of jeans into their backpacks to change from the outfit they wore to school in the girls' bathroom, hoping their parents won't find out. And they are surely supposed to arrive home to the safety of those same parents after their bus ride home each day. Those are the supposed-to-be dreams of middle school girls. They were just not the realities for Amber.

It all began on November 29, 2005 with a phone call at my home. I was already in bed at 9:30 p.m., shot with the typical exhaustion that a middle school day brings. The director of transportation from the school district called to inform me, the principal, that I had a student from my school that had not made it home yet.

*Seriously?* I thought. *This late and she is not home? Come on. What trouble must she be getting herself into? It's cold outside. Her parents must be beside themselves with worry.*

The questions of liability and whether we had neglected attention in some sort of way came immediately to the accountability side of my head. The worry of her safety, however, fluttered in my heart in the other direction. Surely, though, I would see her in the morning, entering the school building like I always would when a student came up missing for a while after school. Panic would turn to relief, and the new day would bring on another list of challenges.

Panic resurfaced by eight o'clock in the morning when the calls began to pour in that Amber never did arrive at home and there was no sign of her at school. Often, when middle school kids run away, they will show up at school to be with their friends. Not today. Not at Beveridge Magnet School. Not with Amber Harris.

The back and forth thoughts rustled my brain like a boxing match with hopeful and helpless punches. Side to side, my head whirled with a range of thoughts from what would surely turn out to be a happy ending, to the absolute worst of what so very horribly could be. Still, I had to portray a demeanor of strength and positivity for all of the worried students and frantic teachers who feared only the worst of possibilities. These emotions, on the other hand, were not close to those of the emotions that the Harris family was experiencing.

The investigation began. Detectives spent days interviewing Amber's friends, classmates, and teachers about the possibilities of where she might have gone, hoping to find the lead that would break the case and hopefully find her safe.

Our school felt like the threatening interrogation room in a scene from *Law and Order*, with real life teenagers treated like possible suspects in a missing person's case. I was the one who had to deal with the feelings of worry and fear from the kids, believing the cops thought they had something to do with Amber's disappearance.

"Did Amber ever fight with her parents? Did she ever tell you she had a boyfriend she was keeping a secret about? Come on, you were her best friend. She must have told you something we need to know." Little girls would leave the detectives sobbing, having felt pressured to tell truths they really didn't know.

I was the one to tackle the anger from the parents who felt violated that their minor children were being called out of class to be interviewed about something so serious without them present. While trying to explain our need to cooperate with the police, I was frustrated with the determined detectives for violating the protection of what a school was supposed to provide.

"How dare you let the police talk to my son at school without calling me?" I would hear, as if I was in control of a police investigation.

By day two, the story of Amber Harris was on every news station, every front page edition of the Omaha World Herald, and was beginning to get national attention. I did multiple interviews about what kind of student she was, how her classmates were reacting to her disappearance, and how the school community was responding to the situation. It got to the point where I requested that the reporters from every station come for interviews at the same time, finally minimizing the number of times in one day that I participated. Thankfully, our school district's media person was able to manage the chaos of the media circus for me.

Every waking moment of my existence was consumed with trying to balance the media attention with the care and attention to Amber's family, to the need to maintain the necessary day-to-day functions of a school. And what about my own need to be a mom to my own daughter in the midst of this 24/7 script? I couldn't forget about her needs, and I didn't. In fact, going home to her each day took on a different level of love and appreciation for the pure blessing of her existence since the disappearance of Amber. And again, all this pressure felt by me seemed selfish to even acknowledge when I witnessed the stress the Harris family was living.

Days turned into weeks with no leads, but enormous support and encouragement from people around the city was felt everywhere. The church community held vigil after vigil. I attended every one of them and to my own amazement and with confidence in my own beliefs, I began to feel such great assurance that there was nothing so powerful as the strength of the human faith in God to bring this precious child back to her family, especially with the numbers in which the prayers were coming.

The private prayers of my own, as I rested my head on my own pillow at the end of every day, were simple and quiet, asking God to provide proof of his miracles with her safe return. The very public, crowded vigils deserve quite a different description.

The black community was by far the most aggressive in their prayer vigilance, with every major church in Amber's neighborhood providing their own opportunity to gather all of God's disciples to the same place with the same task: to pray for God's deliverance of Amber's safety and the strength of her family to hold on to the faith that it would happen.

I often stood as one of the few white faces in a neighborhood parking lot or in the middle of a church pew at an address

I never knew existed. With each event, I became absorbed in the power of faith and belief that her return would indeed be granted.

The vibrations were extraordinary. There were more than fifty human beings locked together like a chain of magnificent force, arm in arm, eyes closed, some with their head's bowed and others with faces and arms raised toward the heavens. I would sometimes open my eyes with a secretive peek, but only for a moment to endure the visual of what my other senses felt and heard. I was perfectly aware that closed eyes during prayer was the unwritten rule, but hopeful of forgiveness in my selfish curiosity.

Sometimes, an uncomfortable jolt of awkwardness in the unfamiliar ways of worship would creep into my being and I'd momentarily get an anxious temptation to run. With those spurts of doubting—"Do I belong here?"—I was always rescued by the comforting touch of a hand or the gentle grasp of my shoulder from some stranger beside me who meant with full intention to make me feel welcomed and appreciated. My awkwardness relaxed. It was as if they fully understood what it was like to be in a crowded place but still feel alone. It was always to say, "We're glad you're here. You're one of us tonight. We love you like we love one another." Awkwardness turned to safety with those gestures of kindness.

With cultural differences seeming unimportant, and a realization of sameness amongst us, Amber had brought the whole community together in her crisis. Church vigils like these filled the month of November and filled us all with hope.

December brought about a community search for Amber on one cold wintery Saturday morning in the neighborhood in which she lived. People gathered to form small groups to participate in an organized effort to scan the area for information about her possible whereabouts or clues that might lead to anything revealing where she had been—a search for her body, a search for clues. Mobs of people gathered to a site where one man led

5

all of us in how to do this task that he had obviously managed before, unlike the rest of us.

I did not know anyone in my group before that day, but I was sure in the end, we would forever be bonded with this activity we had all committed to join together for. James, Michael, and Mirium were neighborhood residents who walked to the site of where our search began. Henry was the farmer who showed up in his camouflaged bib overalls, driving his rusty Chevy pickup, looking like he, ironically, was on a hunt. Charles was the rich white lawyer who came with his wife and kids. They pulled up in their Mercedes SUV and probably looked suspicious to observers who weren't aware of what was going on that morning.

"Why?" I asked Charles. "Because my wife and I have followed this story in the news. We'd hope that people would show up for us if it happened to one of our kids."

I joined a mix of people from around the city and surrounding area with nothing in common but our purpose. For once, there were no separations between races and classes and it felt like everyone was on the same team. Everyone was there with like souls and what felt like the same genuine hearts. I marvel at the mystery of how a tragedy can make this happen in temporary spurts of time in our society, but why not with permanence in our everyday experience? Why does it take a 9/11 or an Amber Harris to bring about such oneness?

We knocked on the doors of dilapidated homes that, for any other reason, would never be approached unless one knew its residents. We shared flyers that radiated the innocence of Amber, her ponytail hanging loosely to her shoulder, resting on her soft pink sweater and the big hoop earrings she wore for the picture day of her middle school yearbook photo.

I trudged through vacant lots, overgrown with weeds, frozen in the wintery weather, and littered with remnants of other people's lives. Empty pop cans, discarded couches, and the scatter of broken liquor bottles that I envisioned told the stories of someone's broken dreams. I walked cautiously around them.

My gloved hands scavenged through trash bags filled with nasty garbage, hoping desperately to find anything amongst the stench that might reveal a piece of evidence that would reveal a hint of Amber's whereabouts. Nothing, after hours of searching, nothing but other people's discarded junk.

Other people's junk also brought about the first break in the case when Amber's backpack suddenly showed up in a trash barrel just two blocks from her home. It contained a notebook with Amber's writings from her English class with her name in lavender ink, while juvenile red hearts and yellow smiley faces sprawled the cover of the spiral journal—the handwriting of a thirteen-year-old girl and the doodles of her spirit: hearts and smiley faces. Found as evidence on Valentine's Day, red hearts brought sweetheart thoughts to us all as reminders of this beloved child.

This missing child became adored and loved, even to people who did not know her. At school one day in April, a woman I did not know entered my school and asked to speak to the principal. She carried a box into my office and assumed an almost uneasy shyness about her, but managed to introduce herself as Margaret. Margaret was soft-spoken and rushed in her explanation of what was in the box and why she needed to drop it off to me. I soon discovered the truth behind her uneasy demeanor was really a front for being humble and not wanting any amount of accolades for what she was about to present.

"I don't know how to find the Harris family and I have seen you on the news, so I thought I'd count on you to deliver this gift to them."

"Oh, how nice of you. What is in the box?" I asked with curiosity, trying to warm her up to more of a conversation and less of a situation that felt like, "Here. Take this. Give it to them, please."

"Just something I made," she said, illusive and mysterious about its contents. I had to probe a little deeper and finally just got nosey. After all, I thought I had better take a look at whatever

7

the mystery box held before I passed it on to the family and make sure it was an appropriate gesture.

"Can I see it, Margaret?" I asked.

"Sure. It's all right. Let me untie the ribbon for you," she said, finally exhibiting a willingness to participate deeper in the presentation.

Margaret's hands resembled those of my grandmother, soft with large veins showing her years, yet aged and worn indicating hard work. She unwrapped the box's ribbon, lifted the lid, and pulled away the tissue paper that revealed the most magnificent colored fabric. She pulled what turned out to be a quilt from the box and unveiled a color replica of Amber Marie's photo, the same one that had been posted over billboards and news stories, milk cartons, and posters for the past three months.

My hands went immediately to cover my mouth, awestruck and speechless. I took time to absorb the magnitude of what the gesture meant: this stranger, taking a photo and turning it into this quilted piece of art, to forever adorn the wall of the Harris home and commemorate Amber. I couldn't help but wonder: would it be a symbol of Amber's safe return, or a keepsake of her memory?

Margaret lowered her head with bashful discomfort, unable to handle the praise. She wanted no glory, no recognition, only the assurance that the gift would be delivered. She left as mysteriously as she entered, never to be heard from again.

I did deliver the gift to the Harrises as Margaret requested. Mrs. Harris raised her hands to her mouth, just like I had, speechless.

On May 19, in the middle of a shopping trip, my phone rang and I listened to the caller break the news that Amber's body had been found. I gasped with a sense of immediacy to find air. The tears began to well and cloud my vision. I blinked and they dripped down my cheeks, smearing my makeup and spotting the fabric of my blouse. My body felt a surge of temperature change like the flu.

Grief took on a sound from my throat and other shoppers stopped like voyeurs and stared with inquisition and helplessness. Their eyes moved from mine to each other's to see what was wrong with the lady taking the call that so obviously revealed bad news. Without uttering a word, they asked each other, "What can we do for her?"

I felt the comfort of a kind stranger, a woman whose motherly hand so gently touched my shoulder and whose endearing face read, "I will stay here, my dear, if you need me to." My inability to stand still, walking restlessly back and forth, brushed her past me, not as rejection, but as a frantic response to mean only, "Thank you, but not now." After I hung up the phone, I turned to find that same kind face, ready for her solace, but she was gone. I felt regret and I hoped she hadn't seen me as ungrateful.

I had to make the call to the Harris family to express my sympathy, but I dreaded it more than any call I'd ever made. When she picked up the phone and took my call, Amber's mom let out a raw, intense shriek that came deep from her gut. I've never heard anything like it. This cry was different. This was a sound that could only be the official, violent loss of a child pain that cannot be prepared for and cannot be predicted. For this mother, her months of vigilant search, putting every ounce of energy in finding her daughter came to a screeching halt on that awful day in May.

All of that family's focused energy to find Amber would soon shift to a refocused determination to find her killer and bring him to justice. The next several months did just that when the rapist and murderer was arrested and convicted for the crimes. An entire year brought about the facts of the man's history, and what exactly took place that cold night in November of 2005.

Charged, brought to trial, and convicted was a monster, Roy Ellis Jr. The conviction revealed the gruesome details that a horror film divulges. The kidnapping, rape, strangulation, and blunt force trauma with a hammer to a little girl, were the heinous particulars that forever labeled him, *monster*.

With the death sentence, Amber's mom said, "Ellis received his first-class ticket to hell."

One might ask, "Where is the *hope* in this story?" Hope comes from a belief that things will turn out for the best. How does a story about a beautiful young girl whose end of life unfolded like Amber's, have any business in a book about hope? What do the two have anything to do with each other?

Hope in the Amber Marie Harris story comes from the responses of human beings to her tragedy. From the moment it was determined she was missing, to the moment in which her body was laid to rest, the hope of humanity surfacing at its very best was revealed.

Kindred souls emerged throughout our community to create hope that all of humanity would watch closer for the innocent souls of all our children. Through Amber's tragedy, a watchfulness of not just our own but each other's children became a reminder of our duties as a society. Amber taught us that what we want for our own, we must want for others. Hope comes through Amber in the belief that all future bus rides home will turn out for the best.

# Chapter 2

## BRIANNA—NOTHING IS EVER AS SIMPLE AS IT SEEMS

Beginning the school year as the new principal of my high school was a greater challenge with the student body than I had ever imagined. Change is always difficult, but I was confident that because of my history as a middle school principal, combined with my experience as a successful teacher and assistant principal, the kids would simply embrace me as the new leader of their school and I would transition with ease. Kids had always, in my twenty-six years in the school system, responded to me so positively.

Oh, how naïve I was in this case. The student body did not greet me with open arms. They did not welcome my presence as the new queen on the block with a vision and a passion for great new things for my new school—our school. They did not show me an ounce of love. Instead, they resented new rules I put in place as a result of feedback I'd received from the staff, the parents, and the community in regards to a climate that had over the years gone awry and was described to me by many as a place where the kids had taken over the school. The student body wanted their old principal back and they were not shy to express it.

Why had I left the warm and safe little world I had established at my middle school? Why had I agreed to take on this new challenge and start from scratch, the task of developing relationships with these 1,800 high school kids? What had

I gotten myself into? Would I find any student happy that I was there?

Enter Brianna. Brianna was a student I spotted on day one of my tenure at my new school. She stood by herself, sat by herself, walked by herself, and literally went about her own business without communication with anyone. At a glance, Brianna appeared to be at school only because she had to be. She didn't appear to have any interest in making friends or socializing with any of her peers, and was absent of a smile every time I saw her.

My first interaction with Brianna was, "Good morning. Can I get you to put your phone away for me?"

Our teachers were frustrated with the lack of meat in the existing rule that students were not to have their cell phones out, so I had committed to pushing for better enforcement of that rule. Brianna kept walking, and though she did not verbally respond, she did indeed put her phone in her pocket.

A few passing periods later, I saw Brianna nearby with her phone out again so I approached her, and this time said, "Now I asked you earlier to put your phone away, and I see it is out again." Brianna rolled her eyes at me, but again put the phone in her pocket and walked on to her next class.

The third interaction, and the one which brought about my first actual verbal feedback from Brianna, sounded something like this, as I sat across from her at the cafeteria table in which she sat eating alone, reading a text on her cell phone:

"You know, I've asked you twice to put your cell phone away, and I see that you have it out once again. Now I'm going to have to ask you to give it to me and you can come get it from me later."

"Fuck you. I'm just sittin' here minding my own fuckin' business, and you're gonna come over here and fuckin' bother me about my fuckin' phone? You're not gettin' my fuckin' phone, so you might as well get the fuck away from me." (The *f* word used as every possible form of speech in the English grammatical world.)

"How about if you come upstairs with me and we talk privately about this?"

"I'm not fucking going anywhere with you."

I knew that probably asking her name was not going to get me anywhere. So I simply went over to the cafeteria clerk, able to see every student's name on her cash register, and asked her the young lady's identity. I proceeded to my office where I called home to share with the parent what had happened.

Leave her in the cafeteria after cussing out her principal? Yes. Make her think that she had won a battle and controlled the situation? Yes. None of this was urgent enough to cause what would have no doubt been an escalated, ugly scene, disrupting the cafeteria and creating an audience, because I wanted to get her out of there right away. The power struggle did not need to go down like that. It was soon enough that I reached her home, shared the story, and informed the adult that Brianna was suspended overnight and would not be able to return without a conference with her and her parent.

Nothing is ever as simple as it seems. A few mornings after the incident occurred, Brianna and her foster mother (*Ah! Foster care. There might be more to Brianna's story,* I thought.) reported for the conference I had requested. When I asked Brianna to share with me what the issue was really about— because it was surely not about the cell phone—she eventually opened up and revealed the whole bucket of realities in her life, which painted a picture that reflected nothing that even closely resembled simple.

Briana's story began with the fact that she has two children that she drops off at daycare every morning and has to be able to contact the babysitter whenever she needs to, therefore the need to have easy access to her cell phone. Her foster care placement came after a series of domestic situations with her own mother. There were stays at the County Youth Center, probation, and this was her third high school she attended as she'd been kicked out of the others. She was deficient in her credits and should have already graduated, based on her age.

Brianna had a story that put the reality of the cell phone issue into perspective for me. Truly, that cell phone was an essential need for this young mother. Truly, it was only Brianna's response to my request that needed some work. And clearly, Brianna needed the help of her principal and our school.

She softened like butter when I assured her that having her cell phone was perfectly fine with me, but if she needed to use it, all she had to do was come to one of us to assist her. I had to convince her that she could trust that our school staff was here to help her. Trust of school people was not something Brianna had on her experience vest. She needed to understand that there was nothing too big to handle, and that all she had to do was ask. This came to a surprise to her.

We came to an agreement. She understood that responding to those who really wanted to do what was right for her in the way in which she responded to me in the cafeteria was not the most effective way to start a relationship. We talked about how she could have better communicated her reasons for needing her phone and what the likely outcome would have been as a result.

After the conference, Brianna and I were as cool as I could ever have wished for. Beginning every day after that with a good morning when she got off the bus, pleasantries in the hallway where she and I clearly acknowledged each other's presence, and periodic visits to my office where Brianna even began to ask me for advice, were the outcome of our relationship that began with such a storm.

*Nothing* is as simple as it first appears. We must take the time to peel back the layers and find out the real reasons that our students might lash out. We cannot take outbursts personally and must remember that we are the adults and must maintain calm, even when it might be so tempting to explode on a student for how they have responded to what might even be a simple and reasonable request. Power struggles do not create healthy relationships with kids and sometimes the adults have to model with patience how they can be avoided. Joy. Hope. Love.

# Chapter 3

# CHOOSING WHICH MOUNTAINS TO CLIMB (THOSE DREADED CELL PHONES)

Sometimes, as a school leader, you have to admit when you are wrong and back off issues that you once saw as so important and that in perspective, really are not. Sometimes, as well, those same issues you feel in your leadership are the ones that you need to back away from are the ones your staff wishes you would not.

The cell phone dilemma is one of those topics that continue to be a sliver in the sides of all constituents in the school community and one that I often get disagreement about in terms of why I've backed off from the initial commitment to my teachers to bring meat to the rule of taking them from kids. I have come to believe it's just not a mountain we need to climb in order to manage our overall school climate. I have begun to put the management of the cell phone, as a disruption to the learning atmosphere, on the teachers as a tool of classroom management and the reasons for backing off the rule are many.

The reality of cell phone ownership in this country has gone from a frill to a necessity in most American homes. This includes the homes of the wealthy and the homes of those living in poverty. This includes the homes of black, white, Latino, and every other culture functioning as productive Americans in this country. Cell phones are here and not going away. In fact, every day a different company comes out with a new phone and markets more advanced functions to make our lives more efficient. Smart phones have cameras, video recorders, e-mail, and texting

16

capabilities. Cell phones have replaced the need for a computer for many people who can literally do all of their business from the convenience of their four-inch phones. So, in this world of daily technological advances and with the responsibility of our schools to prepare our students to function in that world, are we really smart to ban them from the use of such tools? Let's be smarter. Let's teach them how to use those tools appropriately within the school setting. Let's do it with boundaries.

Should kids be able to have their cell phones out, texting their friends across the classroom? Of course not. Teachers must manage the rules of their use within their own classrooms. In our school particularly—an Information Technology Magnet School—don't we send a message of confusion to kids about what technology provides us when we ban them from using it? We should not be so wishy-washy in our messages.

Student cell phones at my school have provided me an awesome opportunity to connect with kids and purposefully empower them to be leaders in making our school a safe and secure environment. I have begun to give my own cell phone number out to students freely with the message that they can text me at any time with any information that might need to be reported to the administration. It's not that I put the number in the newsletter or over the morning's public announcement system each day, but I regularly give it to individual students that I work with one-on-one and see an opportunity for empowerment and leadership.

"Wow. I have Ms. Riggs's cell number. She gave it to me to use whenever I need to inform her of something that will help make my school a better place."

All of the students in my Principal's Student Advisory Group have my cell number. No one has ever abused the privilege of having it. Many have used it exactly the way I intended it to be used. Regularly, information comes to me, which enables school administration to prevent something from happening before it ever has a chance to happen. Students never have to worry about being seen as the dreaded snitch they so often express in discussions about sharing information with school officials. They don't have to be seen going into an office and be fearful of any retaliation.

Our school resource police officer says often how grateful she is that I have put this practice into place, as she is sure our school is safer because of it. She mentions stories shared with her security resource officer colleagues and the challenges they have in their own schools, which she believes are mostly absent at ours.

Some of my own colleagues across the district think I'm crazy. When we discussed as a group the challenges with cell phones in school and it came up that, perhaps, we should tighten the rules on cell phone use in the district's Code of Conduct, I shared how I have benefitted from the tool. I understand how cell phones have caused horrible panic at times when students send mass texts that create potential chaos. I haven't experienced that. I believe I haven't, however, because we have begun to show students that the tool must be used responsibly if it's going to be allowed.

The tightening of the cell phone rule in the Code of Conduct should be harsher for those who use it in ways that do cause chaos. Let's be real, though. We have much bigger issues in urban education than spending the amount of energy it would take, as some would like, to chase down every kid who has a cell phone out in the open. Let the students have cell phones. Tell them to put the phones away when it's disruptive to the particular setting. Allow them to use them when it's not. Empower the students to be responsible. Treat them like young adults and get over the reality that perhaps what really bothers us about students with cell phones is more about letting go of power. Kids appreciate boundaries. Why not create them around the cell phone issue, too?

# Chapter 4

## JESUS—WHO IS THE MOST IMPORTANT PERSON IN A LITTLE GIRL'S LIFE?

Jesus was another student whose first interaction with the new principal was nasty and unfriendly, to say the least. Again, after asking a reasonable question like, "Where are you fellas supposed to be? The bell has rung—let's get to class," Jesus reacted with, "Who are you tellin' me where I'm supposed to be?"

I told him I was his new principal and that I'd appreciate it if he moved on to his class. My demeanor was calm but firm. His nonverbals were as negative as his verbals, scrunching up his face, raising his eyebrows, and moving his head up and down, letting me know he didn't care who I was. Jesus had a very distinct hairstyle: cut very short on top and kept very long on the bottom. At first glance, Jesus looked like the media's image of a dangerous gangster who might, in first impression, tell me he was a force in the school that could be trouble.

After he moved along and eventually landed in his class after the tardy bell, I ran into one of the school deans and I described Jesus and asked if she knew his name. She did immediately and I shared with her his reaction to me. She was shocked. She said that Jesus is normally a very pleasant young man and that she simply could not believe we were talking about the same kid.

Unbeknownst to me, the dean called him in to her office and told him that she heard about how he treated the new principal earlier in the day. To my very pleasant surprise, at dismissal,

Jesus approached me and said in a very sincere manner, "Miss, I'm sorry for the way I treated you earlier in the day and I wanted you to know that you didn't deserve that, and that you won't ever see that from me again."

*You have got to be kidding,* I thought to myself. How could this be the same kid whose words and demeanor just a few hours earlier could have smacked me in the face if his fists would have been balled up? Where did those amazing social skills come from?

"Wow. I appreciate that. What is your name?"

"My name is Jesus, Miss."

"Well, Jesus, I accept your apology and I look forward to getting to know you better."

Amazing. What a testimony that we cannot judge a book by its cover.

The next day at dismissal, Jesus was already outside when I arrived at my supervision post. He was holding the most beautiful little girl I had ever seen.

I walked up to him and said, "Jesus, who is this precious little angel?"

"My daughter," he said with such pride. "I just took her to the doctor and we're picking up her mother from school."

"Jesus," I asked, "do you know who the most important person in a little girl's life is?"

Jesus quickly answered, "Her mother?"

"No," I said, "it's her daddy. You know why?"

Jesus looked quizzically and shocked that the answer was not her mother.

"It's because as women, we seek out men that remind us of our daddies."

Jesus smiled and seemed to truly absorb the magnitude of that statement and the responsibility of what it meant.

"So what that means for you, Jesus, is that you always have to ask yourself, 'am I the kind of man that I want my daughter to choose someday?'"

20

Jesus and I continued to bond over the love he had for his daughter and the kind and thoughtful way in which he treated her mother. It didn't take much for Jesus to learn that who he originally thought was a new, bossy principal just trying to tell him what to do, was perhaps someone who cared enough about him to get to know the young man underneath the crazy hair and gangster look. He even became a quick ally of the new principal and would often stick up for me when some of his buddies had their own struggles accepting the leadership change.

"Who's the most important person in a little girl's life?" I'd ask him as I passed him at his cafeteria table.

"Her daddy," he'd answer with new enthusiasm and purpose every time it came up.

I know he'll be a fine example of what his daughter will look for in a man some day. Joy. A love story. A little girl's lifelong love story. A daddy who shows her love.

# Chapter 5

## ANGEL—SUNSHINE IN THE STRUGGLES OF LIFE

Shortly after I began working at my new high school, I received an e-mail from a student who did not initially want to identify himself. His e-mail to me went something like this:

"Dear Ms. Riggs,

I can tell you are trying to make our school a safe place to be so I thought I would tell you that you have some gang problems around the school when everybody gets out. There are gang members that drive around the school and just try to start stuff with kids. I appreciate that you're trying to make our school a better place. I came from California where the black and Hispanic gangs fought all the time and it was dangerous."

He didn't sign his name and his e-mail did not identify who he was. After corresponding back and forth via e-mail for a while, I talked him in to telling me his name and allowing me to meet with him.

Angel was his name. I had a pass sent for Angel to the main office and he was brought to my office through a door that did not reveal he was visiting with the principal. Angel shared what he knew about the gangs in our neighborhood. He knew so much that I confronted him about my concerns that perhaps he was or had been involved himself. How would someone not involved know so much? He assured me that in his community, everyone was in the know about gang involvement and that at his last school, he was often associated with a gang because his cousin was, and his cousin was really his only associate at that school.

Angel agreed to continue to keep me informed about what he knew to be happening around the school and around the neighborhood and I agreed to keep our contacts confidential. Soon, like with others, I shared my cell phone number with Angel so he could text me with information he felt I should have immediately. There were many incidents that never happened because Angel gave me a heads-up. As a team, we responded and were ready before anything went down. The incidents ranged from fights that were to occur in certain locations at certain times, to food fights, to mass texts that had gone out indicating an all-school pajama day.

From potentially no big deal, to potentially very disastrous, Angel's information was critical to improving our school climate. Protecting Angel with the anonymity was something I was committed to; however, as time went on, it was less important to Angel that I pretend I didn't know him.

Soon, Angel would acknowledge me in the hallways with a, "Hey, Ms. Riggs."

He began to warm up and not be so concerned that his peers notice he actually knew me. Occasionally, I would even get a text from him over the weekend where he revealed some of the troubles he was experiencing with his family outside of school.

I learned that Angel, at seventeen, was the man of his house. His father abandoned his family. His family owned a business, and he not only went to school, but worked at that establishment many hours a week. His girlfriend had been kicked out of her home, and she and their baby now lived in his house with his mother and siblings. One of his siblings, who also attended our school, was terminally ill and in need of a second kidney transplant. Hospitalizations and struggles with the bureaucratic mess that went along with immigration issues were a constant in his family, and much of the burden and the need for strength and perseverance were driven by his seventeen-year-old soul. How could one young man have so much energy to do the right thing? Never in my career had I witnessed such evidence right in front of me that our kids need us so much to show them support and encourage them with greatness.

In Angel's case, greatness was in his DNA. He had it in him to be great. Inspiring him with constant messages of praise and a regular dose of lifting him up was what I was responsible to do. I'll never forget the conversation I had with him about college. This incredible young man never believed he could ever go to college. He believed that because of his citizenship situation, he would never be able to attend. He had dreams about it but did not believe any college would ever accept him. He lived in constant fear of deportation, like many of the students in my school. If I could have drawn a picture of his face when he realized there was indeed hope that he could attend college and pursue bigger dreams, the portrait would have beautiful rays of orange and red sunshine bouncing from his being. Angel was sunshine. He was his family's sunshine. He was his daughter's sunshine. He was my sunshine.

As a school, we needed to provide some sunshine to Angel's family. With his brother's medical challenges, Angel's family incurred crazy levels of medical expenses. I couldn't imagine how even the basics were able to be taken care of when the constant pressure of hospital bills continued to rise astronomically. Though medical expenses were far more than our school could tackle, there were certainly ways that Angel's school family could step in and assist his family with raising funds to pay for things like groceries, gas, and other home expenses.

I had a very active Principal's Advisory Committee, which consisted of student leaders who were committed to taking on projects that bettered their community and school and the students and staff who were part of it. I shared the information with them that they had a classmate—in fact, three at the time—who was in a medical emergency, and that the family was struggling to pay for basic expenses. I watched in complete amazement as this incredible group of the school's student leaders took over the conversation with strategic plans to raise money, not just for Angel's family but the other two as well. I sat back and watched the cream rise to the top in this group; the plan of attack would eventually raise about two thousand dollars per family in just a few short months. These kids took buckets around their cafeteria during every lunch hour, and encouraged all of their peers to throw in quarters and dollars, every single school day. They were at every scheduled event, from parent-teacher conferences to every athletic event and concert that happened during the remainder of the school year. They were determined to help their classmates, no matter how it interfered with their own busy schedules.

Angel learned the power of blessings that come from reaching out. He reached out to help his school become a better place, and others reached out to him.

Angel graduated from high school and is now attending the local community college pursuing a career in criminal justice. Hope has come to fruition for Angel. He believes he can be the kind of man he's dreamed of being, and he is continuing to move toward that goal. Angel is a love story.

Angel tells his own story of his experience at our school. Shortly after his graduation, I received the following e-mail, a bit different from the first one he sent just two short years before. It reads:

"Dear Ms. Riggs:

When I first asked to get transferred to South High, I was going there with the expectations that it was just another high school that I was being forced to go to. When I first got here, I wasn't the best student. I ditched.

I wouldn't do my homework, and I would constantly be tardy. In the other high schools that I attended, the teachers really wouldn't care or make a big deal about my behavior, but here at South, most of my teachers reached out to me. They treated me the way they would treat their top students. These connections that teachers at South gave to students like me, made me want to do well in school and actually stay, instead of ditching. It made me feel welcomed.

Slowly, I went from a failing student to a student with low *Ds* and *Cs*. When my third year at South came, and I got to know more teachers and you, Ms. Riggs, my grades got better. Soon, I had *Cs* and *Bs*. What was supposed to be my junior year was really like my freshman year because I only had freshman credits. The staff helped me stay on track. They constantly checked up on me to make sure I wasn't failing. In my old school, (out of the district) they would not give you a choice about what classes a student wanted. They just assigned them. Here at South, it was different. It was very diverse. I got to meet many different people and learned about different cultures. Thanks to you and South High, I graduated. South High felt like a second home to me.

Before South High, getting up for school was so disappointing. I was only going somewhere I didn't want to be, but at South it was no big deal to get up. I looked forward to seeing what the day had in store for me. South was the best high school that I attended and the only high school that showed me support and love. You and the staff at South made me feel like a friend before a student.

South High is the reason why I'm attending college at the moment. After I graduated, I had decided I didn't want to continue my education due to personal issues, but you kept in touch with me and constantly reminded me about the opportunities I could have if I did attend college. Soon, I was back at South High after graduation and you helped me sign up for scholarships and helped me make appointments so I could get signed up at the local community college. I got my scholarship with you and South High's help and now I'm back in school. I'm so thankful.

Without South, I would have never thought of continuing my education. I will always be a Packer and I'm proud to be a South High graduate.

Thank you, from the bottom of my heart,

Angel Garcia."

Our superintendent, John Mackiel, always says, "Not everything that counts, counts." Angel is an example of that statement. He's a fifth-year graduate who survived the most extraordinary of circumstances that count in the reasons why we as his school family work so hard to ensure that he'll be such an incredible contributor to our society. But in the guidelines of our federal government, Angel counts only as a dropout because it took five years to get it done. It's a travesty. It's a shame. It's ridiculous. We think Angel counts as a success story. We know we did *not* leave this child behind. Angel is a love story.

# Chapter 6

## N.A.S.T.Y. NATE

"My name is NASTY Nate. That's what I go by for this music. NASTY stands for 'Never Ashamed, Stay True to Yourself' Nate."

True to himself is exactly who Nate is. A judgmental person might first look at Nate through ignorant eyes and see what he raps about: "bummy-looking, nappy-headed, and probably never graduate." Hair unkempt and always in need of a fresh cut, clothes wrinkled, he is the kind of young man who the average person walks by quickly with fear and trepidation because they live by stereotypes. To not take the time to look beyond the exterior of Nate means to cheat oneself out of the privilege of knowing him. He is deep, to the level you wonder when he received his philosophy degree. He is thoughtful and caring at a level you'd package for others if only you could. He is ambitious and visionary to the point where you're convinced he'll succeed in whatever he goes after. Nate is a literal sponge for knowledge and new information, soaking up experience and wisdom that others who give him the opportunity are willing to share with him. To not take the time to peel back the layers of Nate means one misses out on the gift of knowing this brilliant young man. His story is one that magnifies the power of hope.

It's a story too common for many of our young African American males: An absent father who left his kids and their mother, only to start another family and begin a new life, erasing the contact with his first family; a mother with her own issues;

a grandmother stepping up to raise Nate. For years, it was Grandma and Nate.

The home was a revolving door over the years for uncles, aunts, and cousins needing a place to stay and put food in their stomachs. No one but Nate really helped to stabilize the home. Arguments ensued over time, and all but Nate would come and go. Nate always stayed.

Nate and Grandma were a team. They took care of each other. When Grandma became ill and the house became run-down, Nate stayed and took responsibility for the one who showed him the most love throughout the years. He took charge of matters that no young teenage boy should have to be responsible for. Nate took care of the rat problem in the basement.

His responsibilities at home took a toll on the progress of Nate's education. He often missed large portions of the school day, dropping in, dropping out, and dropping in again—always, however, with graduation in the forefront of his heart, no matter how long it would take.

I was Nate's middle school principal and was thrilled to reunite with him when I was moved to his high school. It became clear to me early on that Nate's struggles at home required extra support and encouragement from his school family. Music was his passion, along with poetry writing and his amazing desire to fill his own brain with the wisdom and knowledge and the experiences of others.

Nate connected with school through his band instructor who also turned him on to the school's recording studio. Soon, regardless of the continued challenges of caring for his ailing grandmother, Nate's attendance improved. It was Nate's involvement in our Greatness Academy and the magnetic connection between Nate, the other participants, and the director of the program, Wes Hall, that tipped the boat in gaining Nate that desire and perseverance to believe in himself and his gifts, which led him to his graduating with the class of 2010.

It wasn't easy for him, and in the midst of all of the end-of-the-year deadlines and typical stressors that go along with every senior trying to finish up, Nate's grandmother took a turn for the worse. Nate found her collapsed and incoherent when he came home one day. He continued to be the man of the house and put his adult hat on with her hospitalization and rehabilitation stays.

Teachers and counselors and I rallied to assist him in whatever it took to be his family. We drove him to visits to the hospital. We made sure he had food at his home. We made sure his grandmother took part in his graduation celebration, if only getting him to her room in the facility in which she was being cared for to see her baby in his cap and gown and take photos with him holding his diploma. We made sure his hand was held through the application process of our local community college.

Nate's speech at the year's end Greatness Academy banquet included his recitation of the award-winning poem he wrote for a local poetry slam contest, in which his English teacher had entered him. He also took the time to say, "I want to thank Wes Hall, Ms. Riggs, and all of my teachers at South High who believed in me and helped me through all my struggles and to be the man I am today. The Greatness Academy was that object that I hit against that was bigger than myself and helped me get on the course that I'm on now, and I want to thank everyone in the Greatness Academy for that."

His ability to express himself and his sincerity of gratitude could be a lesson to so many adults. There is so much he could teach those adults who see him as scary and miss out on his greatness.

We cannot ever underestimate the potential in any Nate who is present around us. To create opportunities for hope and greatness is our responsibility and should be the mission that we strive for in all of our kids, especially the ones who might appear on the outside to be hopeless. Nate's five year existence as a high school student may have technically, according to the state and federal graduation rate guidelines for No Child Left

Behind, classified him as a dropout and hurt our graduation rate at South, but we choose to celebrate him. We call Nate a success story. We say we did *not* leave Nate behind, regardless of what the rules say.

# Chapter 7

## DANTE—THE SHORT FUSE

Junior year and Dante has been kicked out of another district high school and placed at my school. He approached me right away and said, "Ms. Riggs, don't you remember me?"

I couldn't believe the physical change in Dante since his middle school years with me; his name was as clear in my memory as could be, but the face and physique had completely stumped me.

We moved quickly to my office to pull out the middle school yearbook and shared laughs over how we both looked in our photos back then. My hair was short and an awful red. His body was round and chubby. Both of us were embarrassed by the historical photos of our pasts. We pinky-swore that neither of us would ever show those photos to anyone at our new school, with an, "I won't tell on you if you don't tell on me" agreement. A familiar face created a comfort for both of us in our new settings.

It was not long after his enrollment at South, however, that my memories of his middle school issues where he was in constant conflict with peers and adults came back, for they began to come to the surface quickly with his—what seemed to be—terminal case of short fuse disease.

Once again, I found myself dealing with the same young man I'd dealt with four years ago. His body less round and more muscular, his voice much deeper and masculine, but the issues were the same. The next two years would prove to be a game of getting Dante graduated and a constant challenge to find evidence that he would show some growth in how to respond to people and situations in ways that would not be so detrimental to his success in life. Did he graduate? Yes. Was there evidence of growth in how he responds? Not much. His stories of ineffective responses to things out of his control were always detrimental to his well-being. I worry with great consternation that Dante will be killed someday as a result of his short fuse. The wrong place, with the wrong kind of person, and the deeply engrained value of never letting anyone punk him out could easily kill Dante.

I believe the most powerful formula for life is an equation I wish I could give one person the credit for, as I use it with adults, students, and try to live it myself. The equation, taught to me many years ago by someone else and presented originally by someone anonymous, is $E + R = O$. The E stands for an event in which we have no control. The R stands for the response we give to the event and something we have all the control over. The O is the outcome, a direct result of the response we've chosen to act upon. The R always determines the O. This formula, as simple and powerful as I know it to be, could solve all of the short fuse issues that Dante exhibits in his life. If he could just get a grip on how he responds to people and situations in which he has no control in a way that gives him an outcome that doesn't hurt him or anyone else, life would be simpler and more successful for him, I'm sure. If only it were that simple. Dante understands the formula. He struggles, however, to pause and think out his responses, based on years and years of lashing out both verbally and physically. Following the factors in an equation when approaching life and the situations and people that life presents us is easier said than done.

I recall the day that Dante and a friend had been truant and were brought back to school in a cruiser by two police officers. I walked into the office when the officers were reporting the situation to Dante's assistant principal. I observed the situation where one of the officers was rude, sarcastic, and editorialized throughout his explanation of what happened, revealing what many African American young people say happens in dealing with cops on a daily basis.

Dante was rude and sarcastic back. He paced the office and postured as he remained mouthy with the officer. I feared the officer would soon put Dante in handcuffs and take him away.

I offered to take Dante out of that office and into my own, with the purpose of separating the power-tripping police officer and the teenager who had no respect for his authority and wasn't afraid of the consequences. The officer was happy to have me take Dante off his hands. As we walked out of the office and Dante continued to posture and show his anger through his verbal rampage, we walked past our Greatness Academy director, Wes Hall, and Wes witnessed what he feared was Dante's anger toward me.

"Everything all right, Ms. Riggs?" Wes asked.

Dante, not knowing Mr. Hall and perceiving his questioning as nosiness said, "Was I talking to you, mother fucker?"

I nodded to Wes that everything was okay and continued my escort of Dante to my own office where I knew I could calm him down. I always could. Wes walked into my outer office and I decided to take advantage of his presence and invite him in to, hopefully, do his magic with Dante. I introduced them both to the other as my friend.

"Wes, meet my friend, Dante. Dante, this is my friend, Wes."

Wes extended his hand to Dante, and he accepted the gesture like I'd hoped. I sat back and listened, observed, and watched Wes indeed do his magic. There was nothing in my own experience as a white female—and certainly not the time to bring up $E + R = O$—that could have matched what unveiled between Wes and Dante, as two black males in their experiences with cops. Dante went from explosive and volatile to calm and attentive throughout his attention to Wes's own experiences as a black man with white police officers.

Truthfully, Wes's message and advice to Dante mirrored the $E + R = O$ formula, with Wes's own explanations of the differences in his own outcomes based on how he responded to the various events he faced with officers like the one Dante just witnessed. Nothing Ms. Riggs could have said matched the effect that Wes Hall had on Dante that day.

Sometimes we must reach out to those that can do magic better than we can. My job was to provide Dante with understanding and familiarity, if not from my own voice, then from someone else's.

It was just two weeks until the seniors' last day, and Dante was escorted out of a classroom with another student with whom he'd been arguing. Again, Dante created a scene down the steps and in the hallway on his way to the office. Again, I happened to walk up on his rampage, which this time included a cuss-out and a nonverbal posturing that clearly challenged a security guard to fight him. Again, I rescued Dante from any further repercussions by moving him away from the scene and into my office. As always, Dante soon calmed down, agreed that he was out of line in his response, and even acknowledged, without my prompting, that he owed that security guard an apology.

Wow. I couldn't have asked for clearer evidence that Dante got it, and the suggestion that he apologize came from him, not me. I explained to Dante that I would be designing some kind of independent study for him the last two weeks of school as a consequence for his behavior, in an effort to get him across the stage to graduate. He agreed and wanted to apologize to the security guard before he left. I called for him by radio and asked him to join Dante and me in my office.

As soon as he entered my office, Dante rose to his feet and like an adult who has chosen to humbly admit his own error, he put out his hand and said, "Man, I owe you an apology." My heart raced with joy and pride like a mama does when her child rides his bike for the first time without the training wheels.

The security guard, instead of taking Dante's hand, threw his own hands in the air and said, "Nope. I can't accept your apology."

Mama's heart went from pride to complete devastation and anger, as if watching her child be hit by a car on that same first bike ride.

"Are you kidding me, Ron?" I blurted in horror.

"Naw. Fuck that. I'm not beggin' your ass to accept my apology," raged Dante, immediately back at the level he'd entered my office to begin with.

We went from level ten to zero and back to a level ten in intensity as quickly as a firecracker explodes after being hit with a match. I quickly dismissed Ron from my office and right in front of Dante, let him know that *he* was the one who was now in the wrong, not Dante. So my lesson to Dante after Ron was gone? Even when we do the right thing, sometimes others do not. Dante dug down deep to do the right thing and showed me the evidence that he was indeed learning. Ron pushed him into a corner and took away the glory of what it feels like to give an appropriate response. Dante had practiced $E + R = O$, and though it didn't appear to him immediately, the formula worked, as the new issue was the behavior of the security guard, not him. Damn. It's so hard sometimes when adults don't do the right thing. Still. A love story.

# Chapter 8

## LET THEM LAUGH AT YOU AND THEY WILL LAUGH WITH YOU

There is so much joy and excitement in an urban school, if you only allow yourself to truly be a part of the kids. It requires making intentional time to get to know them as individuals, to get to know their families, to understand their cultures and the backgrounds from which they come. As the principal of a school of 1,800 students, I am blessed with the opportunity of being able to fill myself with the experiences of diversity that go far beyond black and white, from a rich neighborhood or a poor one. The statistical, federally defined subgroups that categorize diversity and point out achievement gaps limit one's scope of who our kids really are if we let it.

The knowledge and understanding of who they really are comes only from learning what their experiences have been. Learning what their dreams are can expose the truth that some of them have not been allowed—or allowed themselves—to dream. True understanding of our kids comes easiest when we allow them to know us as well. It is only when they learn of our own experiences, weaknesses, mistakes, and personalities that they fully allow us into their worlds. It happens in that order. Reach out to them, and they will reach back to you, opening up their gates so the flood of possibilities can be visualized, pursued, and come to fruition.

Allowing students to know us should come naturally. Educators make huge mistakes in their work if they do not have relationship building at the top of their priority list when it comes to ensuring student success and creating an emotionally safe atmosphere of learning. I am convinced that academic achievement does not come for students absent of positive relationships with adults. I don't care how well a teacher is prepared to teach the content of physics; without the ability to engage students through relationships, the physics just won't be learned.

Relationships with kids comes from our knowing that we have to be willing to put down our own fences and allow kids to see us as people first. That is difficult for some educators to do—difficult because some don't think it is necessary for kids to know them as people. That's a shame. When they believe they are only there for the subject matter, they limit the depth of the students' experiences in that classroom and in that school.

It is also difficult because some educators feel too vulnerable at the thought of allowing kids to see their own imperfections. Those vulnerabilities should be dealt with, if we want to truly connect with kids and find the joy from making a difference because we've allowed them in.

Humor with kids is a great way to start breaking down barriers. That may sound scary to someone who does not see himself as funny. Being funny to kids, however, does not mean that you need a body of jokes that make them laugh, because they will laugh at us for who we are if we let them. Go ahead and let them. It really is simple, if we allow ourselves to be laughed at. It's not about trying to be funny when we're not. Please don't. That can be a disaster. Allowing them to find what's funny about us invites us into their world through their acceptance of us. It allows them to connect with us on their terms. It's amazing the connections that can be made through the experience of humor and laughter.

Students often find humor in the language that I use. They see me as corny and dorky and basically just old in my level of what is hip to them. When I stop kids from swearing out loud and refer to it as their potty mouths, kids see that as silly in the language I use. They laugh at me, and I catch them mocking me by using my own terms with others: "Hey, John, watch your potty mouth!" might be heard from a student to another because I'm observing and they know that's the term I use.

"I know, Ms. Riggs. Go find some greatness!" as I walk by students moving in the hallways because they hear me say that to them all of the time.

"Stop playing around over here. We have visitors in the building today and we're acting raggedy!" My black students think that is hilarious for some reason, when I describe unruly behavior as raggedy. I don't need to know why and they don't need to tell me why. They simply connect with me through language. "Come on, y'all. Ms. Riggs says were actin' raggedy, so knock it off!"

I may be the boss, but I've allowed the kids to know me beyond my business suits. On Fridays, our staff wears jeans. Kids think that's cool to see their principal and teachers in jeans, like real people. They know me beyond the car I drive up into the principal's parking spot. They know me beyond the times they watch, as I observe their teachers' performance in their classrooms and beyond the times I have to discipline them for behaviors that do not fit within the norms of the school. They know me beyond the all-school assemblies where I highlight the rules and expectations of the school. These are the basics: the things about me that any kid could find evident about any principal.

What do they know about me because I've allowed them to learn it, and what arenas afford me the opportunity to expose the bits and pieces about myself where kids can truly know Ms. Riggs? The content of who they get to know is as varied as the arenas in which they experience me. When a group of girls sitting together at the same table every day in the cafeteria—a group I always take time to visit with—called me over one day to investigate their curiosities about my marital status, it went something like this:

"Ms. Riggs? Are you married?"

"No, I'm divorced," I answered.

"Oh, well, how would you like to date my dad? Can I give him your number? I think he'd like you, and he's good lookin'! You're a thoroughbred, and he likes thoroughbreds! He just got out of jail, but he's a good guy and I think you two should kick it."

The table laughed and I smiled, connecting with those girls who really got a rise out of the possibility of their principal dating one of their fathers. I knew there were compliments somewhere in those questions and those proposals these girls had put out there to me. I could have dismissed their questions as inappropriate and responded how one in a power struggle might respond, with them feeling like I thought I was too good for her dad (which often educators are good at: making kids feel like they are inferior) but in order to connect, I had to give them a response that made them believe I was real, too.

"Wow. A thoroughbred? Thanks for the offer, Hailey, but I just can't be out there dating any of my students' dads now, can I? How would that look?"

We all laughed and the girls believed that maybe I would have considered it if Hailey's dad wasn't the father of one of my students. That funny discussion connected that table of girls and me every day in the cafeteria, and every time I ran into them throughout the school. They saw me as real and not fake, which is so important to kids. Adults have to be real to them. They can spot fake from a mile away. Love stories.

# Chapter 9

## CREATE CONNECTIONS—DON'T WAIT FOR THEM TO COME TO YOU

Minimal opportunities exist to get to know students fully and allow them to know you within the confines of your office. When I first came to South High School, one student told her teacher, "Is someone going to tell that new principal that she's got an office she can hang out in? Everywhere I go, there she is. If I'm on the first floor, she's there. If I'm on the fifth floor, she's there, too. She's even in the cafeteria during my lunchtime!"

I put myself with purpose in situations where kids are. Hallways are where kids move from one class to the other, so that's where you'll find me. Classrooms, stages, and athletic facilities are where kids are, so that's where I'll be found. Out by the buses at dismissal is where kids scurry to end their days, so that's where you'll find me. The cafeteria is where kids share social time and conversations, so that's where you'll find me. At clubs where kids gather with like interests and missions are, that's where you'll find me. Anywhere where they are, is where I might be found. These opportunities allow me to make real connections with kids. I seek them out strategically. Never would I want a student to graduate from my school with the feeling that they didn't know their principal.

Getting into the classrooms creates huge opportunities for a principal to get to know the kids in the school, not just as an observer, but actually as the teacher. Principals come into school administration with their own content area specialties, as we were all once classroom teachers ourselves. What better way to connect again with kids than to offer our time in a classroom? It is so easy to say we don't have the time to do this, but the dividends are so great, I strongly recommend it.

As a former English teacher, I often craved the occasion to get back into the classroom and reunite with kids again through writing and literature, genres that lend themselves so easily to all of the ways that great teachers engage kids and build bridges with them through the process of learning. When I learned that one of my very favorite novels was on the approved reading list of the sophomore English curriculum, I jumped at the chance to offer my services to one of our teachers and teach a section for her. The truth is the offer came to her for my own selfish reasons. She agreed, and for four weeks each school year, I blocked out one period of my day to teach Sue Monk Kidd's, *The Secret Life of Bees*, to an amazing group of tenth graders to whom I will forever feel connected through this experience. It also provided me the extraordinary chance to practice the strategies that I ask my teachers use in their own instructions.

Let me tell you, it was not as easy as my cocky self thought it would be. I was a great teacher. I loved the novel. What else was there? Oh, my. I learned quickly, first hand, that loving a novel wasn't enough to turn kids on to it. I needed to make it relevant and engage them in ways that made them want to run home and read the chapters I had assigned.

Structured and focused planning, relevancy, high student engagement, cooperative learning, higher-level thinking, etc. were all strategies I led teachers to use. These were practices noted by all of the great researchers on best practices in instructional strategies, but I was still challenged to make them effective in my own preparation of the return to teaching.

*The Secret Life of Bees* takes place after the Civil Rights Movement and includes themes and topics that easily engage kids in some very in-depth conversations and allow them to look inside their own lives and their own experiences.

The relevancy came naturally through the content of the story. The main character is a fourteen-year-old girl with an abusive father. She struggles with the death of her mother, with feelings of abandonment, and experiences the realities of racism, the power of forgiveness, and the strength of friendships and love.

It was amazing how honest and frank these sophomores were willing to be in their discussions and their writing when it came to similar stories they related to with the issues in the novel. When talking about the theme of forgiveness, I shared my personal story of losing my father to the hands of a neglectful surgeon, the wrongful death suit our family went through to seek justice and closure, and the question of whether I had forgiven the surgeon when he never acknowledged wrongdoing, even after the process concluded that he made such lethal mistakes and was held accountable through the system. The faces of these teenagers as they listened to the details of my plight were stoic and thoughtful. The sincere care and concern for what happened came out in their comments. They were split in their thoughts of whether I should forgive or not. We connected. We connected forever or at least throughout the tenure of their high school years, and I knew it.

The sharing of my loss brought out the sharing of some of their own losses and whether or not forgiveness was necessary in their own stories of betrayal, loss, and pain. The real-life theme of kids abandoned by their fathers was rampant in the room of twenty-four students. The loss of a friend through gang violence was shared several times. The sadness and anger toward mothers whose bigger concern, according to the feelings these girls shared, was their attention to boyfriends instead of their focus on their children. Loss, despair, and hopelessness were sentiments our kids in this small class of twenty-four shared unanimously.

One assignment was to write to someone they always wanted to express something to, but had not been brave enough to follow through with. (This was similar to the letter I wrote to the surgeon who took my dad's life, and also to the main character in the novel we read.) I told them to begin the letter with, "Dear So-and-So, I write this letter to you, with the purpose of getting something off my chest." To my amazement, this prompt created immediate focus, with all students on task and writing with vigor. No one in the room had writer's block. It gave me goose bumps to look around the room and see the power of the pen before my eyes. Our kids do have something to say. All of them had issues they wanted to get off their chests. The letters would likely not ever be given to the intended, but getting them to express themselves and explore their feelings was my purpose.

Below are samples of the deep troubles existing in so many of our kids. There were many that were similar, indicating that so many had common strife and tribulations they spent their young lives internalizing, but never expressed them through writing. All of the themes acknowledge that what our students struggle with as young people could likely knock an adult right over the ledge of functioning, and yet they still show up for school and still have the hope of learning and bettering themselves. See what some of my students revealed about their own lives through this simple prompt in the format of a personal letter:

"Dear Dad,

I write this letter with the purpose of getting something off my chest. Why did you leave us? There is so much I wanted to say to you but you left without me having the opportunity. How could you leave my mom and your kids for another woman and her kids? Could they be more important to you than us? Really? I hate you for doing this to our family and I want you to know I will *never* forgive you. Ever.

Love,
Your daughter"

"Dear Sandy,

I write this letter with the purpose of getting some things off my chest. First off, I would like to say that you need to give me my dad's stuff back because that should have been mine when he passed away. Or you could at least give me my stuff he had when he was living there. Oh, and I would like my dad's dog back because I don't think you should have a dog like that because you won't treat her right.

Love,
Marcus"

"Dear Dad,

I write this letter with the purpose of getting some things off my chest. I forgive you for drinking, but not when you lose control. I try and try to make things work out between us, and the family. Well you and I both know that both of us are too much alike. We'll have our arguments and fun times, too. I get angry easy and want to fight any asshole that pisses me off, because that's how you do it. Now, about getting drunk, I know it's the beer talking and taking over, so it don't bother me. I know you want me to be afraid of you, but to be honest, I'm not. All I wish is for you to believe in me. When I get home and get to bed, I am exhausted. I'm tired. I just want things to be better between us. I'll be less tired.

Your son,
Jake

P.S. I still want you to know that I love you."

"Dear Boss,

I write this letter to you, with the purpose of getting some things off my chest. I feel that when I work for you, you are lazy and cheap and no good. I think you've never given me a raise because of my skin color. You know I work harder than anyone else. Is it because I'm Mexican? Well, that's how you make me feel.

From,
Miguel"

"Dear Doctors of Children's' Hospital,

I write this letter with the purpose of getting some things off my chest. I just wanted to let you know that my sister died at your hospital a year ago. I am not blaming any of the doctors that were trying to help my sister. I just can't help wondering if maybe, on that day of March 3, 2009, you guys could have done something more for her. You guys said you couldn't do anything else for her. Now, those words are stuck in my head forever. 'There's nothing more we can do for her.' Those words are haunting my head all day long. Will they haunt me forever? What should I do to make the words go away? Maybe you know.

Sincerely,
Paula"

"Dear Killers in Mexico,

I write this letter to you with the purpose of getting some things off my chest. You probably don't know my daddy. Why did you do it? He was the soul of my life.

He has no reason to be where he is right now. The truth is, if you knew me, you would probably know that I hate you and think of you as trash. That's why I would never forgive you, even though you try to give me money. Money will go away fast. My dad could have stayed and lived longer, but after you did it, he went away fast as if he were money.

Sincerely,
The person who hates you most"

"Dear You,

I write this letter to you with the purpose of getting some things off my chest. The thing that bothers me the most is that you think you are in control of me and you are not. I hate it when you go on telling me what I came here to do in this world and what my destiny is. For once, I would like to be in control of my own life and to find out for myself about my destiny. I hate it that you force me to do things I know I will not accomplish and then you're disappointed when I don't. I hate the fact that you yell at me for no good reason. I always do what you ask and yet, you wonder why I yell at you back? You taught me how to yell. (I just want you to know that I will never yell at my own kids when I have them someday.) For once, I would like to hear, 'Good job, Mija!' or 'You're doing great,' or 'Let's practice so you can improve better.' Not the opposite of that because it sucks not having you support me. I despise the fact that you always prefer money or beer to me and the family.

Sincerely,
Me

P.S. I feel better already because I have said it to you."

"Dear Mom,

I write this letter to you with the purpose of getting some things off my chest. I really want you to understand that often I've been thinking of my dad and what it would be like if I knew him. Now that I'm older, I think I would understand how he or even I would react to it. I like it when you tell me things about him. When you tell me about him, I feel as if he were here with me, but he's not. Some days I wish you would say, 'It's time to meet your dad,' but it's never happened. I hate when you tell me your story about what happened with you and my dad. If he wanted me, why did you run off with someone else? I can't imagine how my brothers and sisters must feel like, actually having their dad around. When I see them happy with their own dad I feel left out because I don't feel like that with him. He's nice, but he's not my dad. The blanket I have of Bambi is the only thing I have of my dad's and that's why I don't ever let it go.

Sincerely,
Elizabeth"

"Dear Susie,

I write this letter to you, with the purpose of getting some things off my chest. You are freaking stupid and I wish my dad had never met you. I went into you dating my dad with a positive attitude that you would make him happy. Well, you don't! And just so you know and because I'm being completely honest, I do not like you at all and I never will. How dare you tell a fifteen-year-old girl she is fat and ugly? You are forty years old. Grow up and stop being pissed about your own high school years. It's not my fault that you were anorexic and no guys liked you. I am not like that at all. I eat, and maybe if you would have then you may have had some friends, too. Bye,

MaryBeth

P.S. And one more thing: don't *ever* try to say you love my dad more than I do again, 'cause you don't."

"Dear Anna,

I write this letter to you, with the purpose of getting some things off my chest. Remember we played together like crazy with our Barbies and I would spend the night a lot on the weekends? Well, I do, and I miss that so much. We would tell each other our dreams and say we would be the first ones to go to college in the family. What happened to that? I know I will get it done. I am in school and taking honors' classes to accomplish our dream. How about you? I hate that you met that older guy. I hate him. He changed you. I hate it so much that you got into trouble and dropped out of school. You know I haven't seen you in three or four years. You are in Mexico now with your new son. I know his name. You probably don't know, but I cry at night because I need you back. What happened to your dream?

Love,
Lizza"

I saw and felt the abandonment, loss, fear, and confusion. I left that classroom, each day for four weeks, feeling like I knew twenty-four more South High kids better than I ever would have if I'd not engaged in the opportunity to teach them. I knew, as well, that this particular group of twenty-four was only a microcosm of what my whole student body included in regard

49

to the realities of their worlds. Some days, I'd have kids from my class approach me and want to talk about the reading ahead of class time.

"Please tell me, Ms. Riggs, that what I think is going to happen is really not going to happen," said one girl who got off the bus and ran to me hoping to learn that the fate of a character was not what she was predicting.

"You'll have to wait and see, Rachel! You'll have to wait and see!"

What great joy exists when you can see a child light up through reading and witness the rays of hope bounce from the zippers of their backpacks.

# Chapter 10

# BREAKING GENERATIONAL CURSES THROUGH FOCUSED SCHOOL PROGRAMMING

Generational curses are rampant in urban school settings. How do we make a difference with kids who have seen their parents, aunts, uncles, cousins, and sometimes even grandparents engage in behaviors that are detrimental to positive growth? We are so much of what we see and what we believe to be our only reality. Kids actually download the emotions and reactions they are shown. Without new downloads and the belief and hope that things can be different, our kids repeat what they've seen around them, and what has been accepted and expected as the norm around them. They repeat the involvement of gang ties that go back over decades in some families. Daddy and all of his brothers were OGs (Original Gangsters, longtime members of a gang), so there's no debate on whether Jesse will be Crip or not. They repeat the custom of having a baby—or maybe two—as teenagers: a baby at fifteen just like her mama had her, with the likelihood of grandma raising that same baby so she could go to the clubs at night, just like her mama did when she was a baby, and maybe still is.

Generational curses. History repeating itself. Poverty multiplied with the dead ends of welfare checks and public housing. Substance abuse. Criminal activity. How do we provide our kids with evidence that circumvents everything they've been taught to know as truth? Telling them of the possibilities of hope for change means nothing. Often they're even skeptical of the adults in their schools who try to show them the potentiality in their lives, when we don't look like them and they perceive all of us to be from situations so different from their own. For the most part, they're right.

"You just don't get it, Ms. Riggs. How would you have a clue of what I go through, Ms. Riggs?"

Providing them with real life evidence they can feel, hear, and touch is the only way they'll believe it can be theirs. The evidence must also come from the ability to expose them to others whose stories might be similar to their own and who have overcome those same obstacles with success.

"Show me. Don't tell me." The school can interface with those tangibles that bridge them from the helplessness of what their families experienced to the hope of something better, but not through simply telling them they can. We must show them. Even with strong evidence and the process of them beginning to believe, they may still sabotage the possibilities because they just can't imagine themselves in what they perceive as something make-believe.

For urban kids, telling them to run for student council or try out for the school play is likely not going to be the activity that will connect them with their schools. Unless the student council represents the issues they can relate to, touches them personally, and reflects the makeup of who they are, that meeting will not be of interest to urban children. Unless the school play is an opportunity that provides them with a chance to show their own authentic talents and not those of others they cannot relate to, it will also not be the magnet.

My student principal's advisory committee must reflect the diversity of my school. Again, not just the ethnic diversity, but the Goth kids, the gay students, the athletes, the scholars, the artists, and the techies. All diversity must be seen and recognized as important to the makeup of the school family. All of them need connections to their school and we must be willing to create new connections if we do not have existing ones. Our school has had some success with nontraditional, out-of-the-box programming.

## The Packasso Project

Steven: "Head's spinning, feeling good, thinking life's great. Been painting all night, and no one can stop me. I'm a vandal; I destroy everything, even your building. Wait, who's that coming around the corner? I run, red and blue lights flashing behind me. Her hand on the trigger, yelling, "Stop! And Taze them!" Never polite. My hands are twisted, and my wrist hurts. Light is in my face, and all I can think is: this isn't the first time. How is it going to end this time? The gang unit busts him again. Jail. Probation. An ankle bracelet."

Phillip: "Painting graffiti was my escape from picking up a gun and a rag or grabbing a needle. I saw graffiti as a window—a window of opportunity and freedom. I could climb out this window from the life I was living at home and jump into a whole other dimension. It's like when I jumped out that window and picked up my cans of paint, I felt careless and free. Like I was unstoppable. I went by a different name. I hid in the shadows, and I crept on the rooftops. It's just an indescribable feeling that almost no one else understands."

How do we engage the seemingly most at-risk from dropping out to staying in school, an institution and concept they lost interest in long ago? Our Packasso Project is a great example of how the creation of purposeful programs can create amazing connections for kids who have not been connected to school before.

During a conversation with one of the gang unit officers with whom I worked closely, the topic came up about the tagging problem that is so evident in the community where our school is located. Graffiti is also found around our school occasionally, sometimes in bathrooms, or on the side of the building, appearing overnight. I asked Danny how many of the taggers he catches are enrolled at South High. He said that most of them come from either my school or another high school not too far from ours. We brainstormed about what it would take to make an impact on these graffiti artists, stopping the vandalism within our community and school. I reminded Danny that South High is a Magnet School for Visual and Performing Arts. Why couldn't we create a program, and involve adults interested in contributing and students who are identified by the police department, the school, or any other agency as students involved in, caught, or dabbling in the craft of tagging? We spoke of how the craft is really an amazing art form. Why couldn't we redirect kids and show them what skills they really had and how they could practice them and exhibit them with the support of society, rather than the ultimate punishment from society when it's done as vandalism?

We formed a small group of individuals who helped polish the original idea. We then invited a small group of those targeted kids and we proposed the project to them. All but two stayed around, intrigued by what the project could really mean for them. It was so interesting to watch them enter the room with the group of us who came up with the plan.

Spotting Officer Torres in the room and bringing up the word graffiti put them at an immediate distrust. Why would these parties, a gang unit officer, their principal, and a few other staff and community have anything positive to offer them in regard to their illegal graffiti skills? They really could not believe the proposal as something real. Was this a ploy to get them to admit any of their past crimes? It may be why a few of them did not return. They just couldn't trust the proposal to be real.

Those who stayed, however, were able to craft the project as one in which they would benefit fully. We didn't want the project to be only how we designed it. We wanted their input, too, so that it would insure success for these kids and have some valuable impact and longevity. So began the Packasso Project. (The name was a combination of the South High Packers and of course,

Pablo Picasso.) The beginning is a story by itself; however, the artists who unveiled themselves as a result of the project were the real story, and a testimony to how effective nontraditional programming can be in getting at-risk kids connected with their schools.

Prior to the birth of the Packasso Project, the students who were involved had similar characteristics beyond their desire and involvement in the art form of tagging. None of them attended school on a regular basis, which resulted in the natural credit deficiency toward their graduation requirements. If they did come to school, it was always late, as if they slept in at home and came only, perhaps, because someone was making them. Progress reports in their first quarter of school showed a pattern of failure. It surely wasn't because they couldn't do the work; it was only because they were not coming. Like most kids with poor attendance, the more school they missed, the easier it was to miss. It had almost become shameful to show up when the feedback felt like, "Why are you even here?" What also came along with limited attendance and poor grades came poor attitudes and a visible demeanor of, "I don't care. I don't like you. I don't like me. Leave me alone." These are kids who if no one would have given them an opportunity to engage with school, they never would have. Furthermore, they likely would have engaged in activities—and some were already fully engaged—that were illegal and would have ultimately led to jail time, or worse.

By the end of the school year and into the summer school session, all of the participants in the project were visibly different kids. I say "visibly different" because they were not only visible in their daily attendance, but it was obvious they were feeling differently about themselves. They were smiling. They were making eye contact and acknowledging the adults around them. They appeared to have hoards of friends around them, like other kids just wanted to all-of-a-sudden be around them. Their teachers were absolutely in awe of their changes and became such huge cheerleaders for their new success, praising them daily with the positive accolades that good teachers do naturally when their students are achieving and they are proud of them.

One of the students received the honor of Student of the Month, nominated by one of his teachers who was so proud of his turnaround. That young man would have never seen himself, nor would have his teachers or parents predicted that he would ever be honored at a luncheon for his achievements in school. But now, with the newfound belief in himself as a talented, valuable young man who has a future in art—and we really believe he does!—his daily outlook has done a complete 360 turnaround.

Like Juan, Maria was the same success story. Her situation, prior to the Packasso Project, was even more bleak, as she had some serious emotional issues going on atop the nonattendance, poor grades, and defeated attitude. In fact, a community liaison whom I included in the preliminary planning of the project recommended specifically that we try to get her involved, as he knew some things about her that he was more than worried about. He expressed a concern that if someone didn't do something drastic to intervene in this young lady's life, her safety and her life were definitely at risk. Today, you would never believe she is the same person. You would never believe the details of her life outside of school and how she felt about herself were ever an issue. She is seen at our school as a brilliant artist. We've allowed her work, along with many of our artists, to be exhibited throughout the building, on display for everyone to admire—or not.

A few staff came to me and wanted her work to be taken down because they felt it was inappropriate. I quickly gave them the art speech where art is a personal preference that often tells a story about the artist. Artists don't ask for permission for the audience to like it. We don't appreciate all artwork, and like our trips to museums and galleries, we walk by those pieces we don't immediately feel aesthetically connected to, and that's okay. I explained that though I appreciated their opinions, I needed to remind them that as a Visual Arts Magnet School, we would sometimes push the boundaries. Her work was indeed dark, but I was not going to take it down because a few adults were uncomfortable with it. She got wind of the "controversy" and came down and volunteered her work be removed.

She said, "Ms. Riggs, if people don't like my work, I would be glad to take it down."

I told her, absolutely not. Just because a few folks didn't appreciate her genre didn't mean we would remove it and cheat others out of the experience of her effort. This was part of the experience of being an artist. Some people will like your work, and others will not. She smiled with pride, and I could tell that she felt supported and even more proud of her talents. The easiest thing for me to do would have been to take down her work, and as a result, been safe and not have to ever worry about others getting riled up about it. That would have been the wrong thing, however.

Additionally, Maria stretched her talents in an advanced placement art class. Following the school year, she received her score on the AP exam and immediately called her mentor from the Packasso Project to discuss the score.

"Tell me, what's the lowest score, and what's the highest score you can get on this test?"

The mentor said, "Don't worry about that; just tell me how you did!"

Maria insisted, and they went round and round before Ms. Bishara finally revealed to her that a one was the lowest and a five was the highest, obviously worried that she'd received a one and that Maria would be so crushed.

Maria screamed on the phone and announced, "Oh my God! I got the highest! I got a five!"

The two celebrated and Ms. Bishara proceeded to do what great cheerleaders do for their kids. She marketed the news of

Maria's success. It didn't take long before Maria began to hear from other adults.

"Maria, congratulations on your AP exam score! That's wonderful! We're so proud of you!"

She beamed each time she received that kind of positive feedback, and like every other kid who gets it, it began to be contagious; it began to be something she wanted more of. Her self-motivation and her personal ambitions began to be natural for her. Her future was clear. Her vision of being a successful artist was a truth she believed in—and we believed in, as well—and a reality she no longer doubted.

These students no longer believed the only attention they could get with their art talents were to be done in secret and with the constant reality of being caught and jailed for it. Now, their work on the side of businesses was done because someone contracted them to do so. By the way, the artists in the Packasso Project have indeed begun to get work commissioned by members of the community. They have done several murals within the community on the side of buildings, for individuals on canvas for their own art collections, and recently were asked to professionally tag the side of a barn by a woman about twenty miles away who lives on a farm and wanted real graffiti to decorate it. They've done a barbershop wall, a dance studio, an ice cream truck, a bus, and even their principal's basement wall.

For five hours, eight of the Packasso students spent the day tagging my basement with what turned out to be the most incredible three walls of art I've ever seen. While they were there, the doorbell of my house rang, and I opened the door to a stranger who asked for one of the students. It was his tracker. The student, who was on probation for some prior tagging in the community and monitored by an ankle bracelet, told the tracker he would be at his principal's house doing the tagging. Obviously, the tracker did not believe him and wanted to see for himself. I led the man to the basement where he watched in amazement. He was thrilled to see Steven participating in this legal project that motivated the young man as an artist.

Steven and these kids are connected. They are connected with their school, with their community, and with their own individual futures. South High's Packasso Project was recently presented at two different conferences, one locally, and one in Houston, Texas. Four of the students were able to travel for the first time outside of the city of Omaha and experience the world as a much bigger opportunity. They loved seeing the potential of choices beyond their backyards. Hope.

I cannot emphasize the magnitude of the success of this project because of the adults who made it their personal mission to make sure it worked. Beyond the original committee of organizers, individuals from school spent a great deal of time making sure the project was a success. Ms. Bishara, especially, was the catalyst and the driver of the project. She was always the *go to* for the kids and the real angel who made the project her baby. The relationships she built with these student artists were vital to their success, and we cannot minimize that component when planning successful projects. We cannot believe that without committed adults who follow through with the vision, the projects will not survive. The adult human component and the adult connections with the kids will ultimately make or break the program.

Steven: "The Packasso Project was there for me. It's a way to show everyone I want to change. I have permission walls now to express my art, and I feel I'm going somewhere. These people are helping me explore my artistic ability while showing that graffiti can be harmless and an art form. I'm showing the courts that I'm on a good track and will soon graduate. I'm not sure where I'll be in the next ten years, but I know it's not where I was headed." Steven is registered and headed to college.

Phillip: "Ever since I joined the Packasso Project, I've been on the right path. It saved my life. I know now that there is hope in my community. All these kids need nowadays is a good role model to push them in the right direction in life. That's all it took for me, and now my life is completely turned around and I am on the right path for a bright future and a new beginning. Now I am inspiring other young kids and doing all sorts of things that are good." In his words, "It saved my life."

## South High's School-Community Teen Parenting Program

Upon my arrival at South High Magnet School, I was inundated with a number of local business owners, parents, community leaders, and clergy who were anxious to meet the new principal and express their concerns and hopes for the future of the school. A wonderful minister from across the street visited with me about his church's wishes to be involved in their neighborhood high school and offered to assist in any way possible to help make a difference in the lives of our students. He asked for any ideas I might have that would put them directly involved in the betterment and support of the school.

"As a matter of fact," I said, "there is something your church can do to help." I shared with him the great number of teen parents that existed in the South High family, and what tremendous challenges that presented in not only their school success, but their futures, as well. Immediately, the minister sat back in his chair and looked intensely at me, giving me the initial belief that he was not at all interested in supporting this particular need.

I thought, "Okay, here we go. Will this be one of those people who, under the guise of God, says he wants to help, but then becomes judgmental about who he will help?"

Much to my surprise, his blank and quizzical look of silence was merely his brain going into automatic pilot and reeling with the possibilities to move forward. We shared our beliefs that in order to insure that all students are successful, including the students who face unwanted pregnancies, it was more than time to support them rather than ignore them. For too long, the reality of teen parents in schools has been almost a secret as to the numbers that exist. I believe, as well, that when supporting teen parents, we must not exclude the teen fathers from the equation, as they need and want to be part of the services as well.

Teen pregnancy is an epidemic and must be dealt with more realistically in the early years of schooling. This is very controversial. Nonetheless, it is vital that we stop putting our heads in the sand, or the numbers will not change, and the reality that we deal with the outcome of young people having babies will only get worse. Part of the controversy comes with folks believing it is not the school's responsibility to spend time and resources on anything but educating students. If we continue this attitude, we make it more difficult for this group to succeed as young people, as students, and as parents. The challenges young parents face become so overwhelming that many become dropouts, continuing the cycle of hopelessness.

Schools should be places of hope, where all students, regardless of their current situations, should be given evidence that their lives can be filled with greatness, even when the pathways to it require detours. Pastor Ron agreed and forged ahead with our staff to initiate this cooperative venture between the church and the school to support this group of very needy students and their young children.

Saint Martin's Church and Omaha South High Magnet School began their amazing example of how a public school and a faith-based community can work together to insure success for students. Pastor Ron and his congregation set to work and forged ahead to include agencies in the collaborative efforts to support the teen parents of our school. What started as just an idea manifested to a fully functioning program that allowed all of our teen parents to participate in this support group, which ultimately led to thirty of thirty-one teen parents graduating from high school the very first year of the program's existence.

The church gathered items like diapers, clothing, blankets, books, and toys, which were given to the teen parents who earned baby bucks for all of the time they put into participating in the program. The program included agency instruction that ranged from literacy, dental care, and healthy eating habits to discipline. Mostly, it provided a support group for these young parents who had common struggles and issues they faced.

The more the teen parent attended, the more baby bucks were earned. A full-time, teen parent teacher was added to our staff to give daytime instruction with elective credits and provide support systems to this very special group of students with unique needs. That teacher integrated the church program into the curriculum. Students also earned the coupons for attending study nights where they could do homework and work on computers the church donated. Our school's counseling staff was relentless in the follow-through and collaboration with the church, actually having a key to the red door at the church and escorting the students after school and making sure they got on the late bus if that was what it took. Again, it was an example of success as a result of dedicated staff, putting their names on specific projects as their own.

Though we are not interested in becoming the school district's magnet school for teen parents, we do believe that taking care of our own is something important for us to provide and what all schools should do. Pastor Ron and Saint Martin's Church were awarded our district's A+ Award for their work with our teen parents. It was a beautiful tribute of thanks from the adults who knew how much they deserved the recognition.

## Credit Recovery

Hopelessness is never as evident as when students, for whatever the reasons, fall below grade level because of their failure to keep up with required credits. The despair they feel in trying to imagine being able to catch up their credits so they can walk across the stage and receive their diploma is so great.

"There's no way I'm going to graduate, Ms. Riggs," was a common statement I heard when I became principal.

Students who experienced multiple class failures, and where credits were going to be necessary to redo in order to graduate, were quickly contemplating the reality of dropping out instead of prolonging their high school years. We just couldn't have that. The graduation rate I inherited was low. It was so low that it put our school in the state and federal government's No Child Left Behind category of Persistently Low Achieving School (PLAS). In addition, we just couldn't have that many students walking around feeling hopeless about their futures and fearing the full semester redo of classes they had failed before. What could we do to build hope and allow students a viable, individual new plan, which allowed them to see the end of the graduation tunnel as something reachable and attainable?

"I can do that," was what we needed students to see and believe in. At our school, we decided that online credit recovery was the answer to that prayer of hope for our kids who were behind. These students were already facing school schedules that were full, with every period required for graduation and no more room for the additional credits needed. We knew that it was necessary to provide hours outside of the regular school day to get the job done.

We hoped that students would indeed take advantage of the additional time, warranting the funding it would take to pay staff to supervise the computer lab as support and tutors for the online program. We began to offer this program on Saturday mornings in room 442, a computer lab with thirty computers. To our surprise, we learned quickly that thirty computers were not nearly enough to take on the students who were not only interested, but fully committed to taking advantage of the additional opportunity to earn credits.

One open computer lab turned to two computer labs. Two computer labs led to the opening of the library, as well. All three areas allowed around eighty students, every Saturday morning, to work individually on getting closer to their goal of graduation. Every week, all of the seats were taken. We treated the opportunity as a privilege and connected some strict prerequisites to the ownership of those Saturday seats. Students must have regular attendance during the school week to keep the seat. Students must show up for the Saturday time in order to maintain their status, as well. There truly was a waiting list to be part of the Saturday Credit Recovery Program.

If all of our seats were used on Saturdays, there needed to be additional times in which we offered this program. Soon, we added a zero hour and an after-school time. We even offered some in-school time where a few students could engage in seat time during their study halls. Summer months also created time in which students could catch up. The month of July created the opportunity for another month of full labs where 121 credits were earned the first summer, and 120 the second, allowing several additional students to graduate, and other students to begin the new school year back on grade level.

We were thrilled with the progress, and our students were motivated again to be dedicated students at our school. We knew this would assist us in increasing our graduation rate. With credit recovery and many of the other focused programming we put into place, our graduation rate went up 7 percent. We were thrilled at the progress and knew we were moving toward making our school a place where all students could be successful.

Traditional school is something we knew our school could look nothing like if we were to address the needs of all students. Some students need a late start because they must take their younger siblings to school before they come to school themselves, as their parents are working and there is no one else to take on this family responsibility. We don't say, "No, it's a rule that you start at 7:45 a.m. like everyone else." We say,

"Yes, we can be flexible so that the student starts second period."
When transportation becomes a problem, we seek out bus passes
so students don't miss school. It's really amazing how often
flexibility is just so appreciated by the student and the family.
Something as easy as a late start changes a student's outlook
from, "I can't do this," to "I can do this." Again, with staff who
takes these kinds of projects on as their babies, like Ms. Lagana
and others, the job gets done.

# Chapter 11

## RACINE—SHE CALLS ME MOM

The word *mother* can be defined as, "A woman who acts or is thought of as a female parent, guardian, or provider, giving love and protection." Racine calls me Mom, and I let her, not because of my ego or some hidden desire to take on the task of motherhood to anyone but my own daughter, but because I know that she means it. She does see me as a provider, as someone who gives her love and protection. To tell her not to call me Mom would take away her gesture of endearment and appreciation that she expresses every time she says it. I let her, because she understands the definition of what a mother is supposed to look like, act like, sound like, and treat her daughter as, but she hasn't had that reality in the relationship with her own mother.

Racine's description of her mother is quite different from the experience I was blessed to have with mine. My world of a mother and daughter relationship would seem like a fairy tale, something fictitious and make-believe to Racine. The same characteristics of the healthy and loving relationship I experienced with my mother are now being mirrored in the relationship with my own daughter: probably the same natural process of mirroring that took place between Racine's mom and her mother, as well. Our reflections just look different. We do what we know. Racine's mom is likely doing what she knows in the patterns of parenting that were created for her. Add bipolar disease and alcoholism on top of that, and it's no wonder that Racine searches for outward influences of what she dreams a mother to be.

With my mother, I experienced support, kindness, warmth, affection, love, guidance, inspiration, and affirmation, even when I wasn't at my best. Shouldn't Racine seek out those feelings from someone else if she can't find them from her own mother? I let her call me Mom because she wants to call me Mom. I show her guidance and love, even when she's not at her best. Not at her best is what she shows outwardly at least once a school day, but at her best is what she longs to be. She lacks the skills to achieve this in many situations she faces. I'm sure of that.

Poverty is a condition that brings on challenges greater than any others I can find to diagnose the most detrimental barriers to success. Racine's upbringing in poverty is no different. Her family struggles financially. The adults have trouble keeping jobs. Welfare checks barely pay for the rent and utilities. Our school has sought out funds to help them pay for the electricity to be turned back on and for gift cards to grocery stores for food when their refrigerator is empty two weeks before the next check comes in. Why? Is that the school's job? Probably not by definition, but yes, it is, if we know it's a way in which we can get Racine to not give up and keep coming to school. It means we give her family our lightly worn clothes, rather than donating them to Goodwill. It means we provide her with her own alarm clock so that her sister, who parties too hard most nights and sleeps through the alarm won't keep Racine from catching her bus in the morning to get to school. It means our student council secretly adopts her family for Thanksgiving, after her mom takes off with the turkey in the middle of a family fight, just days before the holiday. In Racine's reality, Mom yells, "Fuck all of y'all!" and runs off with the turkey they were supposed to share as a family.

"Fuck all of y'all"? Is that how mothers talk to their daughters? Is that maybe why Racine has such a fowl mouth at times? But Racine's mom will show up again. She'll return when her sister or boyfriend or neighbor kicks her out, and the cycle will continue. Racine will continue to be exposed to all of those dysfunctional ways in which her family deals with the strife of poverty and struggle.

Racine came from another high school after being kicked out for fighting and continued disrespect to staff. It's not that there haven't been near fights and definite situations where Racine was disrespectful to our staff, as well. In fact, Racine is a daily time bomb, ready to explode at any moment. I know on the mornings that Racine arrives at school with her hair a mess—understanding that perfectly groomed hair is such an important deal for a happy and confident young African American girl—that it's going to be an exceptionally bad day for her. When her hair is a mess, Racine's attitude is a mess. Every time we avoid a code of conduct violation by the mere chance that she asks to go to or gets escorted to the office before it gets too bad, is a huge victory. Each episode, however, takes an amazing amount of work through time. Don't have another student crack on how Racine looks or what she's wearing. Those are ingredients for an ugly confrontation that will demand some intervention. Each hurdle we clear, however, gets us a little bit closer to Racine understanding that she does want to do better and be better for her own future.

I marvel at how Racine can be in the most dangerous of a rage with a deep desire to "kick a bitch's ass" and at the same time be sobbing with tears rolling down her face, wishing she wasn't behaving that way.. Rage and tears flowing at the same time, each emotion flaming the other's intensity. It's so sad to see her torn between the two emotions: the one which she knows so well—the rage—and the one which she doesn't quite understand—the desire to be different. It is so sad to watch, but every bit of time invested is worth it because she has such hope for something else. Sometimes I just want to cradle her like a baby and hold her, and rock her back and forth.

"Shhh. Shhh. It'll be all right."

Racine is part of my love story, no matter what the challenges are that she brings to me. Even when the late night text came to my phone that said, "Ms. Riggs, don't be mad at me, but I'm pregnant. My family thinks I've been snorting white powder and that's why I've been throwing up. I'm not. Please don't be mad at me."

Her fear of disappointment forced her to tell me over a text and not in person. The news came on the Friday of a long weekend. She obviously didn't want to wait to tell me in person. Of course, the news came to me with a response of emotions that I'm glad she didn't have to see or hear in person.

"Oh, no. Damn," I said to myself out loud in the comfort of my own home. Why? I was both angry and sad. With all of the progress she'd made at our school, how could she allow this to happen and put another barrier in her way? I remember the day that her sister came to get her from school to take her to the doctor to get the shot.

"I'm not havin' any babies in my house, so I'm gonna make sure Racine keeps up with her birth control shots," said her sister with this sense of security and a firmness of the matriarch at that home.

I thought at the time how smart that was. The last thing that family needed was to add a baby to the constant challenges of survival they already faced. The last thing Racine needed in her already difficult situation was the responsibility of a little one. The last thing another little baby needed was to enter this world into the realities of financial struggles and other social issues that would likely continue the generational curses of the Johnson home.

And still, I would put on my armor and charge through the situation with the best advisement and support I could muster in this new war before Racine. A mix of war with love was what we have so much practice at in the world of urban education. We fight and we love. That's what we do. Now we add parenthood to the preparation responsibilities for Racine. Graduation must still occur. And teaching appropriate social skills was even more vital and important now that she would become a mother.

69

So much to do, with so little time. I'd need to pray for guidance on this one. Still, Racine remains a love story to me. It would be important for me to be sure she knew that. And we work toward her graduation. Just a few months until she walks across the stage. And just a few more until she delivers her baby—a girl.

# Chapter 12

## TANISHA—HOPEFUL FOR HERMES

Tanisha's mom was my student earlier in my career, when I was an assistant principal. Her mom, Erica, was a handful with huge struggles, and was equally as volatile toward both adults and peers with whom she interacted. I remember, clearly, the frustration Erica's mother continued to have throughout Erica's high school experience. When I learned Tanisha and Erica were mother and daughter, I wasn't surprised, as we truly are our mother's daughters in the qualities we take on as we grow up mirroring behaviors. Tanisha was as beautiful as her mother, Erica, was in high school, seventeen years ago, and as smart as her, too.

Today, Tanisha's introduction into my life came as a result of having been kicked out of her prior school for fighting and having completed her time in an alternative school. Completion of an alternative school setting should mean the development of successful social skills, which enables a young person to thrive in a return to a regular school setting, but too often it does not. Years of bad habits and the realities of what they see and experience and are forced to face outside of school make that hope of change in behavior a great challenge.

Tanisha was no different. Evidence of her volatility showed up quickly upon her arrival at South High and though seventeen years passed since I'd dealt with her mother, the issues I witnessed and faced with Tanisha were familiar. It was helpful, however, in getting Erica to partner with me to work with Tanisha.

She remembered how closely we worked together toward her own success in high school, and therefore a trust began in assisting with her daughter who she indeed wanted to graduate from high school without the drama that had been part of her school experience. And after all, Erica was now a successful adult.

Often, Tanisha showed clear signs of understanding what was right and wrong with the way in which I observed her help others. Several times, Tanisha would bring in friends to my office who were struggling and in crisis and needed a spot to calm down and regroup. Sometimes, they were friends who were crying and upset about their life situations outside of school, perhaps having been revealed on the bus ride to school or overnight via a phone call she'd shared with friends. Other times, they were students who were angry and needing to calm down before they did something to jeopardize their own status at school.

I'd listen to the advice and support Tanisha would give her friends, as she used my office as if it were her own space to conduct her private practice of counseling. I was convinced that Tanisha heard these same words of advice from others, likely her own mother. Usually she reserved this space for her friends to collect themselves, and I'd sit back as an observer only, as her own leadership in the counsel was more powerful than anything I could contribute.

Tanisha knew what to say to others but so often had difficulty practicing what she'd preach. Clear signs of understanding and an ability to apply the understanding to her own reactions to situations were definitely a conflict for Tanisha, but one that frustrated her, as well. She knew what to do. She knew what not to do. She just couldn't control herself in the heat of her emotions before situations occurred, and it was too late for the inevitable consequences that ensued.

One particular day clearly illustrated Tanisha's conflict with what she knew to be right and how she struggled to control her anger.

"Can I get an administrator to the cafeteria, please?" said a desperate-sounding security guard over his radio. "I'm about to have a code one here and need some help!" he restated with more urgency in his voice, as a fight was inevitable in his eyes.

I was already on my way, my high heels only allowing a semi-jog of a pace to respond to his emergency, but I was confident that there would be several others responding to the call in front of me. Indeed, there were several who beat me to the situation, but I immediately became alarmed when I arrived upon the scene and saw that the student creating the unruly commotion was Tanisha. She was wild with adrenaline that was so off the chart that I was sure she would not have a later memory of what she did.

One of the teachers who witnessed the scene later indicated to me that he had never seen a kid so out of control as Tanisha was during this incident. The out-of-control scene was not so much about the other student she had gotten into an argument with, at her cozy cafeteria table that resembled a booth in a fast food restaurant, but the way in which she reacted to the security guards who were trying to get her to leave the booth and be escorted out.

When I arrived and saw that she was screaming at them to, "Keep your mother fuckin' hands off me, nigga!" I directed them immediately to not touch her.

I knew Tanisha. She meant it. You do *not* touch her. "Please do *not* touch her," I repeated more firmly to security as I pushed to get closer to her.

"Tanisha, it's me, Ms. Riggs. Just come with me, please," I said calmly, but with enough volume that she could hear me over her own screaming.

"I don't give a fuck who you are, nigga! I'm not going with you either. Don't touch me, nigga!"

I knew she would come with me, but she was out of control, and I needed to get everybody backed away from the situation to simply allow her to get out of the booth and go on her own.

We didn't need to touch her to get it done. I know that had I not gotten there when I did, the situation would have gone in a direction that could have been disastrous. She would have likely swung on the security guards who were trying to pull her from the booth. That would have led to a massive disruption and possibly multiple incidents if the large number of students who gathered from the lunch hour had gotten involved, as well.

It is not to give myself credit for the outcome and to sound like Superwoman had arrived to be the only one who could have minimized the situation, but the level of intensity required *someone* who knew Tanisha to get her to cooperate. Cooperation is usually about calm negotiation. Calm. Negotiation. Our students are supposed to, in an ideal world, simply follow the redirections of school personnel when they arrive at the scene to get it under control. Why can't we just say, "Stop!" and they stop? In reality, however, many of our students will only do so when they are first feeling respected in how they are approached. Even when their behavior exhibited just prior to the need for redirection was very disrespectful, they must feel respected if they are going to respond to your commands.

To some adults, this is just way too out-of-the-norm of who deserves respect and when indeed respect is necessary to even be comprehended by the adult. "Why should I have to worry about a respectful approach when I have a volatile situation that I have a responsibility to intervene and get under control?" "Why should I have to show the student any bit of respect when they are spewing disrespectful language and are in a rage, ready to swing on someone?" It's truly difficult to get many adults to see otherwise in the logic of this respect issue.

For me, however, if the adults in the school cannot intervene with respect, with calm, even when feeling disrespected, they should not be working in a school setting. The adults have to be able to separate the behavior from the student. That's not to say that the disrespectful child will not have consequences for their actions of disrespect. It is vital that there are consequences when the situation is resolved, the atmosphere is no longer volatile, and the student is rationale enough to understand the logic of why they earned the consequences. To have to deal with an adult who acted inappropriately with their power and acted out their own form of disrespect is contrary to everything we should be modeling.

Back to Tanisha. Within seconds of clearing the path to allow her to exit her cafeteria booth on her own, without the need for any physical contact, she indeed moved quickly out waving her arms, ranting with foul language, and pulling out her phone to dial someone with urgency. I followed quickly behind her, and one of the security guards moved cautiously behind me, obviously close enough in my vicinity if I needed him. I knew I would not need him as soon as I got her somewhere without the natural effects that a large audience always created.

"Tanisha, just come with me . . . walk to my office and we'll talk. We'll work this out; just head to my office," were a few of the requests I made to her, all the while trying to get her out of the hallway and somewhere private.

"Leave me the fuck alone! I'm not going anywhere. I'm gonna get that bitch; where is that bitch?"

Indicating her state of mind in attempting to get calm, she obviously went back to focusing her anger on the girl at the table with her and not on the security guards. Okay. I realized that wasn't working very well, especially when she passed my office door, with no intention of doing as I'd asked, and continued walking with speed to maintain a distance from me.

Past the guidance and counseling offices we went. No luck in encouraging her to take that left. Down the hallway toward an exit was where she was heading. Okay. I guessed she would likely push open the door and sprint out of the school building, the surveillance cameras hopefully revealing the direction in which she'd go, as I was losing my ability to keep up with her.

I was surprised that my one last request to get her to stop worked when I said, "Here, Tanisha. Let me open up the theater doors and we can go in there alone and you can just calm down. I won't say a thing if you don't want me to. Let's just go in here."

She stopped when I took out my keys and unlocked the doors to the theater lobby. The area was dark with only soft lights coming in through the windows of the doors that connected to the street. I dismissed the security guard, nodding to him to leave us alone, that I would be all right. I saw his face, which showed concern and I reassured him with another nod to go, that it would be all right.

The door from the hallway to the theater lobby slammed and it was now only Tanisha and me. No audience of her peers to show off for. Not the girl she had begun the argument with in the first place. No security guards ready to move her, by any means necessary—just Ms. Riggs and Tanisha. I sat in a chair and watched as she paced the length of the lobby, back and forth, back and forth, all the time ranting as if performing to an audience with the most dramatic of scripts written for a screenplay. (It was ironic that we were sitting in the theater lobby.) Had the performance been on a stage, the actress would have surely received a standing ovation. No performance. Just real life emotion. Just raw pain revealed in the passions of her emotions.

I sat in the chair with my legs crossed, perfectly still to the content that I listened to with my head shifting right to left as she passed me every thirty seconds or so, hoping she'd catch my eye to see that I was hearing her story. A story it was, mixed intermittently with evidence of pain from the past and pain from the present. The rage and the tears played a cadence that mirrored the speed in which she walked. All the while, I remained quiet. Every once in a while, Tanisha would look over at me in the midst of her script and say "you know what I mean?" I would nod. I would softly close my eyes to acknowledge an understanding of her story. There needed to be no lecturing. There was not time for advice or any brilliant wisdom I might muster, as it was clear that Tanisha needed to purge the frustrations in her life that she so easily had built a monument to, yet knew, to grow, she'd have to heal.

Tanisha's constant use of the word *nigga* in her messages will need to be explained to most nonblack readers who do not have the cultural proficiency to understand its meaning. As a white female, I can only translate my own interpretation based on my years of observation of its use, and don't claim to own any authentic understanding. I must, however, be willing to look behind the lenses of Tanisha and other African Americans who may use the word. For many, it's offensive.

It's a word that causes a myriad of emotions from the listener. Sometimes the emotion is shame, related to the history of where the word originated. For some, it's anger, also related to the word's originality. The use of the word is one of the most controversial subjects amongst many African Americans when the question is asked, "Is it appropriate to use in the twenty-first century?" Oprah and Jay-Z, for example, have debated openly about the use of the word in rap music, with Oprah conceding to a better understanding but not completely agreeing that it is okay to use. Paper after paper and dissertation after dissertation has been written in the most scholarly of atmospheres to debate the use of the word.

There's no debate, however, that the word *nigger* is never appropriate, as it is clearly only used by white people practicing hatred and prejudice, and probably in denial as to that fact. That word is not what I attempt to explain. *Nigga*, on the other hand, is a word that has been reclaimed by African Americans and a word often heard in the urban setting.

If we listen carefully to how the word is used, we observe various things. It ranges in its use, sometimes even used affectionately, like a substitute for friend, and other times used as a word that criticizes the receiver as if to say, stupid. It has no limits to race or gender. It can be heard as an expletive with something funny. Listen to any famous black comedian and you'll hear it throughout his act. You might hear niggas, representing a whole group. With Tanisha, and the use of the word in all of her angry emotions, she used the word as a substitute for names, instead of other expletives that would have also shown anger.

Whether the listener agrees with its use or not, or whether there are some settings where the word is more accepted than others, it is still an urban vocabulary word that must be understood by those who truly want to understand the students in our school. To understand Tanisha's story, I must understand her fully. Understanding is a step toward getting to a place where kids will accept when a school person redirects them *not* to use the word in the school setting.

Tanisha jumps from one adult to the other as the person she'll go to at school. She only needs one. She only wants one. It's a game she plays, as if to say, "I hate you now. I'll grace this new adult with my presence. I dismiss you." The dismissal comes after too many times of holding Tanisha accountable for her actions. When I appeared to lose patience with Tanisha, who never seemed to give back to the hours and hours of investment I put into her by changing her behaviors, she dismissed me for one of my assistant principals. It's amazing how quickly the relationship went sour.

One day I'm describing the vision I had of her future, the next, she's shut down the dream. I described the lawyer she'd expressed the desire to become with the shiny, black, 7-Series BMW pulling into her underground parking at her high-rise, penthouse apartment in New York City. She gets out of her sleek car, gracefully moving both legs from the inside of the driver's side to the cement floor of the parking garage. She reaches into the backseat to grab her Louis Vitton briefcase to work on a brief for her big prosecution the next day. Her beautiful suit forms to her figure like a glove and her Jimmy Choo shoes match perfectly, probably purchased specifically for that one outfit and worn with no others. She throws her keys into her Hermes handbag.

Her eyes drifted and her head nodded, as if to recall a similar vision she'd had for herself, or to place herself in that scene I'd described. She could see it. She could be it. Her once honors-level classes meant she had the depth of intellect required. Her ability to argue certainly showed potential to be a prosecutor. The times she'd expressed her goal to go on the black college tours.

If only she could control her anger now, the only true barrier standing in her way. She held onto this conversation with Ms. Riggs today. Tomorrow would be different, when she chose to dismiss me of any kind of trust and support after I had to suspend her for another explosive disruption. Onto the next trustee. I was hurt, yes, but I was glad she found another person as she wouldn't survive without one, though she didn't believe that. "I don't need help from nobody!" she'd often say. Her dismissal was tough, I must admit. When she hated you, she was determined to mean it, or at least pretend to show you that she meant it. The roll of the eyes and the jerk of the head, along with the loud-enough-to-hear-it, "She makes me sick" comments to her friends when she passed me were attempts to get me to react to her. She couldn't stand it when I would walk by her and say, "Good morning, Tanisha" or "Glad to see you back, Tanisha." The calmer I stayed about the choice she'd made and the more unmoved by her nastiness to me that I remained, the more it appeared that she showed both verbal and nonverbal disdain for me. The worst was the day I walked up on the disturbance that ultimately got her removed from our school permanently.

"You want to fight, bitch? Come on, we can fight right now!"

I rushed in front of the other student as Tanisha evidently rushed from behind me. The crowd gathered and the shouts of the would-be fighters got louder, one in front of me, and Tanisha behind me. I remember hating the feeling of not being able to see behind me, knowing that Tanisha's aggression could this time put me in danger, along with the girl who she wanted to fight. With every bit of my strength, I moved the other girl into the office to my left, pushing her body with one arm and pulling the door open with my right. Then I stood with the weight of my body on the door so that one could not get out, and Tanisha could not get in. The door was framed around protective glass and I could see Tanisha's face, just inches from where she could see mine. She screamed at the staff to get off her, who had by then gotten a hold of her to stop her from her rage and determination. Our faces were literally smooshed against the glass, eyes directly into each other's. I begged her to calm down as I watch the school police officer have to cuff her to control her.

"Tanisha, calm down, please," said the woman she'd recently dismissed and decided to hate—me. Glass door between us, I felt helpless, her eyes glaring deep into mine with nothing but anger. Or was I reading those eyes wrong? Was there really some hidden plea to save her that I just couldn't read beyond the fight?

The truth is everyone who wanted to help her felt helpless. The girl with the penthouse apartment, the glamorous job, and the car that symbolized success are a dream only she could make happen. A dream she continued to sabotage.

Hope or hopelessness? All of the questions looming regarding her destiny, and still, a love story. Reassigned to yet another school. A mom, too, who once trusted me to "hang in there with her daughter," now angry that I could not.

I believed my heart would always hold a spot for Tanisha and a prayer for victory in finding that penthouse apartment in New York. I would remain hopeful that one day she would come back and say, "Look at me. I did what you said I would." Until that time, however, something inside me said to keep a close eye on the possibility that she could maybe be a danger to me. Time would tell.

That time came sooner than I imagined when Tanisha showed up six months later at a school football game. My heart dropped when I saw her walk with an increased pace as soon as she spotted me leaning on the stadium's fence. I felt fear. I'm sure my feet shifted to brace myself and I gave a quick look around to look to see if I had support if she came charging at me. The fear diminished suddenly, though, when Tanisha put out her arms and her face revealed a gentleness that read, "I'm sorry." We held each other for what seemed like several minutes.

Though Tanisha's school enrollment continued at an alternative school, we continued to have a positive relationship. I even encouraged her to continue her success in her new school, with the promise to allow her to walk across our stage for graduation if she finished up. Hope was witnessed with this young woman who I believe will indeed sport that Hermes bag.

# Chapter 13

# HELPING PARENTS PARENT—
# LOVE STORIES

## Charity and Her Daughter Eaden

Charity and Eaden are multigenerational gang members. Charity spent years being part of the gang life and living the lifestyle that naturally came with it. Alcohol and drugs were commonplace. Charity never graduated from high school; in fact, she dropped out after eighth grade. Fighting anyone who needed to be beaten up was not something Charity ever took time to think about. There certainly was no time to debate whether the fight should occur or not. There was never any time taken to negotiate the pros and cons. You just fight in her world.

Charity wears the scars of her battles. She sports the tattoos that advertise her loyalties to the gang and to the various men she has had over the years. Up and down the hands and arms and vertically across the neck, the tats document Charity's history. She's hard. She's tough. Her vocabulary is full of colorful words that sting one's ears with the cadence of their flow. She's quick to strike out at people with whom she is angry and she is quick to get angry with most people. All of my encounters and witness to the above have been in my dealings with Charity and her daughter Eaden, as the mom and student at my school.

With every incident I have worked through with Charity and Eaden, as ugly as most of them have been, has been hidden a deep desire that Charity has to do better so Eaden's future will look different than her mother's past. Unhealthy and dangerous habits, and a gang culture that is wildly reactive, however, make it difficult for Charity to change, regardless of her want to do so. As a result, Eaden's example is tarnished and any semblance of hope for something better becomes a challenge—and perhaps impossible—to visualize and believe in.

Eaden has gang ties, just like her mother. She claims to not be in the gang, yet all of the evidence says she is. Her associates are all affiliated. Her enemies are either gang members or girlfriends of rival gang members, and her conflicts are always fallouts of both. Charity struggles with what is appropriate and what is not in helping her daughter. When it comes to school, Charity wants Eaden to be successful because she was not. She wants better for Eaden. However, Charity does not know how to coach Eaden to do better than she did, or she would. She does not have the skills to help her work through conflicts any differently than she did. When Eaden had heard for days that there was a group of girls who wanted to fight her, Charity came up to school to report it to me.

She told me, straight out, "If I see those girls in the hallway when I leave this building, Ms. Riggs, they're mine."

I walked her out that day and told her forcefully, I would ban her from the school if she clowned. The threats from the girls toward Eaden evidentially continued, and so Charity finally told Eaden to do what she knew best to do.

"I told her to arrange for the fight to happen behind Burger King and I would take her over there. I didn't want her to do it in school, Ms. Riggs, but she has to do it. She has to show those girls she isn't scared. She's no punk, and they need to know it."

"You can't think I would ever give my approval of this, Charity," I told her.

She really thought I would, because she was sending her daughter the clear message the fighting should not happen at school.

"So let me get this right, Charity. You're going to pick Eaden up from school, put her in your van, drive her to the back of Burger King, and watch, and even cheer her on as she fights these girls?"

"Yes, Ms. Riggs. It just has to be done this way."

"But what about the reality that you don't know how these girls fight and that there is a great possibility there could be weapons involved? How can you count on this fight being with fists only? You can't," I told her, "and you can be assured that when the police show up and hear that you—the adult—were part of the plan that led to the incident where someone got killed, that you will be in jail, too."

The fight never happened, thank God, but only because Charity was willing to listen. She knew what I would say, and I am convinced she wanted me to talk her out of it, to help her process the scenario. It was far-fetched and completely out of the realm of her experience, but I know that she honestly was willing to let it go because she wants nothing more than for her daughter to be okay. She wants to learn the skills. She wants to change her habits. She wants to do better as a mom. Victory, this time.

Next times came often with Charity reaching out in her efforts to parent better. Sometimes we had victories, and sometimes we did not. Sometimes, the victory even came with Charity but was destroyed by Eaden's fear to let Charity be victorious as a parent. Those were the most disheartening to witness.

Charity and I really wanted Eaden to experience the homecoming dance. It was a high school memory that Charity never had. It was a high school memory that I had experienced myself and had watched hundreds of young girls experience with great joy. We both wanted Eaden to have that. We both wanted her to know what it felt like to get dressed up in a beautiful dress, to have her hair done, and to have shoes that matched her gown: to walk with pride, to walk tall, to smile because you know you're at your most beautiful at that very moment, to walk like you're a princess from what you've only seen in a Disney movie. Charity and I had the same hope for that fairy tale experience for Eaden. Money was tight for Charity, but we had help for that.

Our school nurse has collected barely worn and brand new prom and bridesmaid dresses donated from throughout the city to create the most amazing closet of those fairy tale promises for the girls in our school. It's a closet that makes dreams come true before our eyes. When young ladies think they cannot attend an event that requires the pretties they only imagine in their dreams, we can help bring that vision to life for them. To watch them walk out of the dressing room with the rose taffeta or turquoise silk flowing down their bodies for the very first time, is like a photo any mother spends a lifetime fantasizing being a part of. Charity felt that way the day Eaden walked out in the gown she had chosen. It was a Cinderella experience of a different kind but still storybook in dramatics. Cinderella, with the normal garb of khaki, saggin' Dickies, and a navy blue bandana lain carefully outside her pocket, that day walked through the curtain gowned drastically different in silky, cocoa-colored satin. Feminine lace and an oversized bow in the back draped her body like the perfect image out of a bride's magazine. She stood with a clear elegance and femininity never seen in her before, even with the slight hint of a tattoo between her breasts that read, Armondo.

Charity cried for her daughter. I cried for Charity. Eaden smiled, appearing pleased to make us both so happy. The hope of the evening we'd imagined for Eaden stood before us with full evidence that it would happen the way we'd dreamed for her. I rushed to find Eaden the next day at school to share with her the special jewelry and beaded handbag of my own that I'd promised her she could wear to finalize her outfit for the dance, for Cinderella's ball. Everything was perfect. Or so we thought.

The night of the homecoming dance came and hundreds of students poured into the event with their very best attire. Like Eaden, many would walk into the venue having the experience for the very first time. They looked incredible. There was an obvious sense of feeling special from all of them, doing everything they could to catch the eyes of the caring adults as if to say, "Can you believe I'm here and how beautiful I look? Can you believe it's me?"

But where was Eaden? Her mom had already texted me to thank me. She was so happy to report that Eaden looked beautiful when she left the house. Charity did not have a camera to document the occasion, so she asked if I could take a picture of Eaden when she got here so they could have it forever. Of course I would. I watched throughout the night, but Eaden never came, and I had to break her mother's heart and report she was a no-show. Eaden never came because Eaden couldn't put herself into that dream, no matter how much everyone else wanted it for her. She couldn't be the princess dressed up for the ball. She couldn't be someone she wasn't, and why couldn't her mother understand that? Eaden had her own special evening planned. She was in her Dickies getting high with her homies. No victory that night.

Hope would come in other incidents with Eaden and her mother. Though Cinderella gowns would never be part of the fantasy because it was not her own, Eaden never gave up on the dream of graduating from high school. Traditional high school, like the homecoming dance, would never be the pathway to accomplish that dream, but alternative school would. We made sure she found that venue that fit her vision and ultimately became her victory. We never gave up on Eaden, and she didn't give up on herself.

# Chapter 14

## JUST PLAIN FUNNY, LAUGH-OR-YOU-MIGHT-CRY, SHORT LOVE STORIES

After giving Racine several bags of clothes from my own home, she came to school the next day, proud to have on some of my daughter's clothes: jeans, a shirt, and even some jewelry. She also wanted to make sure to let me know that her mom was appreciative of a few items that had been mine. Racine said, "Yeah, my mom said, 'Be sure to tell her thank you, but I didn't know Ms. Riggs had a big ass like me!'" in regard to the pants that fit her.

One day, I wore a skirt to school with no pantyhose. One of my girls pulled me over to her cafeteria table, and in front of all of her friends, pointed to my legs and ankles and said, "Dang, Ms. Riggs, did you know that Ashley Lynn's Tanning Salon has a sale on tanning sessions right now?" The table roared and so did I at her acknowledgement that I seriously needed a tan!

Many years ago, when I was an assistant principal at another school, I intervened to break up a fight between two girls. Like most girl fights, there is a lot of smacking and pulling hair and scratching. They are ugly, and unlike boy fights, go longer than they need to when an adult gets in to end it. The fight was by all means over and the two girls were separated and I was between them. One of the girls decided to take a cheap punch over me to get to the girl one last time. Unfortunately, in the process, she accidently hit me in the nose instead. I went to the ground with a bloody nose. Breaking up a fight just happens quickly, and you don't worry about getting hurt yourself. I was glad that it wasn't one of our teachers who was hurt. The kids who saw the incident were actually angry at the girl who hit me. That was endearing, but not as endearing as one of my boys who returned to school the next day and visited me in my office, having heard about the incident.

"Ms. Riggs, man, I heard you got jacked yesterday!"

"Yes, I did, William. And where were you?"

"Ah, you know I'd have had your back if I'd have been here, Ms. Riggs!"

While deep into the discussion of a chapter from Oliver Twist that I was teaching in sophomore English, I was excited and proud of the level of engagement that my students were contributing to about the content. The room was obviously filled with smart kids who thought and communicated deeply about the themes in the novel and it was a teacher's dream to experience what I was experiencing in our novel analysis. Suddenly, Joseph raised his hand from the seat in the first desk of the middle row. Because of the level of critical depth of everyone else's contribution, I was sure that Joseph was going to have something powerful to say, as well.

"What is that pink thing on your chin, Ms. Riggs?"

"A zit, Joseph, now can we go on?"

"Ah, man, Joseph," said the other kids in the room, completely jumping on him for his lack of cool in what he said. It was a great chuckle.

While teaching a lesson in a first period class, I walked the room during my instruction as I always did. Everywhere I walked, however, I noticed a horrid smell that seemed to follow me with each step I took. Was the smell something in the classroom that I hadn't noticed before? No, the kids would have pointed it out. Is it a student that needed to bathe? It could be, as stinky kids are part of education. If the smell is following me wherever I go, however, could that possibly mean the smell is on me? Oh, my goodness, was it me? I immediately moved my nose to my right shoulder and identified the yucky smell. Inside the cashmere sweater on the shoulder pad, I recognized the strongest aroma of urine I had ever had so close to my nose. The visual then came to my mind, having earlier that morning picked that same sweater up from the floor after it had fallen, evidently, from the top of my dresser. My dog had peed on the shoulder pad of my cashmere sweater, and I wore the sweater to school.

"Ms. Riggs, your breath is kickin!"

This one student, in his brutal honesty, made me always have mints around throughout my workday from then on.

After an angry exchange with school staff from a mother who believed her daughter was being bullied by a group of girls, the mother stormed out of the school building at dismissal. The campus was full of kids exiting the building to get to their buses, and many just standing on the front stairs and sidewalk, waiting on their own rides home. A seemingly quiet and calm dismissal changed quickly, when all of a sudden, seeing the group of girls she believed were the perpetrators of her daughter's ongoing anguish, the furious mom threw expletives toward the group and turned to give them one last message of, "Kiss my ass!" She whipped down her pants to moon not only the group of mean girls, but everyone else in her shot, as well. As they say, "she really showed them!"

"Ms. Riggs," said my secretary in a whisper with a look of angst on her face. "Ms. Douglas is here to see you, and she looks really mad. She said she's got to see you right now."

"Send her in," I said with a brief pause in what I was doing to wonder what it might be that made her mad this time. Ms. Douglas was always mad and it could have been a range of issues that made her go off this day.

Just when I thought I'd heard it all, though, Ms. Douglas said, "Ms. Riggs, you better get my son down here right now. I'm going to beat his ass. He took my weed off my dresser this morning."

"Ms. Douglas. Did you say Jonathan has your weed?"

I stared at her with my mouth agape and my eyes bugged out as if to say, "You're kidding, right? You are really here telling a school official to assist you in the transaction of returning your weed to you, in my office, between you and your son? Am I supposed to allow you to 'beat his ass,' too?"

Sometimes, in the worst part of a day when a principal needs a pick-me-up because without one, she just might not survive the regular chaos of the school day, my own escape for refuge is room 445, the special-needs classroom where some of my favorite students can be found. Some with Down syndrome, others perhaps with autism, and others with learning disabilities that require special adaptations, it's a sure thing that love is in the room. My entrance to this classroom always guarantees me automatic joy and the ability to forget the challenges of the day. Outbursts of, "Ms. Riggs! Ms. Riggs is here!" Smiles so sincere and so beautiful that you wonder why you hadn't come earlier and can't wait until the next time you return. And the hugs. Oh, the hugs. Even when the kids are being taught to keep their hands to themselves, they get special permission to give Ms. Riggs a hug when she comes into the room. Who cares that a hug might result in a tomato smear on the lapel of my expensive suit coat, left over from the spaghetti sauce on the face of one of the kids, a remnant from the day's lunch? Who cares that sharing a giggle might also include a sneeze with a face full of snot and goo that you need to help wipe off the face of an angel?

"And who is our new student who has joined your classroom today?"

The teacher led the new girl over to me to introduce her. I was anxious and excited, as I made it a point to know all of the kids' names in room 445. Another new friend. Another angel.

"Ms. Riggs, this is Brandy," introduced the teacher.

I leaned down and put my hand out to welcome her. So sure of myself. No doubt in my mind that the new girl would love me, just like the other kids in the room.

"Hello, Brandy!" The other kids gathered around us and said, "This is Ms. Riggs," their hands petting my arms as if I were their little puppy they wanted to share with their new friend.

Brandy looked up at me, bright red hair and freckles, and though I just knew she'd be as happy to meet me as I was to meet her, she instead crinkled up her freckled face and with clear enunciation and strong voice said, "*Bitch!*" Oh, my. It seemed to stretch out into more than one syllable. Just clear and strong, "*biiiittttccchhh!*"

So much for the immediate acceptance of my welcome to our school from the new girl!

Oh, the smells one runs into when working in a school. Elementary schools, I'm sure, bring about different smells than do middle and high schools, all representative of hygiene and social changes going on in each grade level's student body. Which level is worse than the other? I'm convinced that the secondary school kids insure a range that cannot be simply put, but is mostly gross to say the least. I literally gag at the rancid smell of the boy running past me from P.E. class who's just finished an hour of full court basketball, sweat so thick only a real scrub down of Lava soap could get rid of. Instead, though, high school boys simply throw their clothes back on and bathe in a quick covering of AXE, the contemporary teen cologne marketed to all the cool studs. The combination of the funky body odor and the cheap cologne brings tears to my eyes and singes my nose hairs.

Then there are the fart kids. The quick whiffs left lingering in your way, thick but not visible, causing you to walk through them like a hidden tornado funnel—no warning and no advanced notice—always, leaving you scared to death that the people behind you will think the mysterious sour smell is your own and that you'll be the focus of pointing and embarrassing but inaccurate and unfair accusations. Every once in awhile, you can avoid walking directly into the fog of student farts by being extra observant. It might happen that the kids ahead of you have already discovered the perpetrator. That's the for sure group that scatters like cockroaches having just been exposed to light. Instead, it's the quick exit of kids yelling in unison, "Ah, Johnnie, that's nasty!" And Johnnie left alone in the middle of what was once a circle, playing dumb and saying, "What?" playing the I-don't-know-what-you're-talking-about role. You avoid that mob of obvious nasty odor, so relieved that you've been forewarned to proceed with caution like the flashing of the yellow light in an intersection.

Then there is the necessary can of bathroom spray that anyone with an office must have close at hand whenever that girl with the smell so foul you just can't begin to guess what the source is. It's likely the reality that some girls just don't bathe enough and then they put on clothes that haven't been washed. It's often that rancid smell of her period. It's the girl that is so bad that you breathe through your mouth instead of your nose, trying everything in your power to not get a second breath of what you already inhaled once. It's the girl that a classroom just cannot function in with her presence. The one that the nurse has tried numerous times to have the talk with. Nothing seems to work. Not gentle, firm, honest, or shameful talks. Nothing. And it's the same girl that seems to always need to visit with the principal. A literal fumigation of the chairs and office air is a must upon her exit before anyone new enters the space.

Or what about the parents who must smoke pack after pack of cigarettes and just can't smell the layers of Marlboro that linger in their presence like a fog? It's awful, and the quick pop of a mint doesn't come close to covering up the smell they think it can. Surely, the home and the car are thick with the constant clouds of smoke that are deep in the fibers and pores of everything and everyone exposed, and remind you of a scene from a Cheech and Chong movie. Sometimes you're tempted to walk the halls with a mask on, therefore fully prepared for the icky smells the day may bring.

The local Burger King restaurant, just two short blocks away from our school's campus, is often a hangout for students not in a hurry to get to school in the morning, and also for those who may escape for what they see as a tastier lunch than what is being served in the school's cafeteria. I will often start my day on a mission to round up kids and clear out the establishment to round up groups that would otherwise be tardy to school. Balancing a full cup of hot coffee, I march down the sidewalk determined to maintain a graceful pace, all dressed up and in my heels, but on a mission to get a job done. It is a skill I've mastered and one that often gets me points and stares like, "What is she doing?"—God forbid if I'd accidentally trip and let anyone see me fall!—by the time I stroll into the BK. It is always a surprise to the kids to see their principal storming into the place, breaking up the breakfast clubs and forcing a quick eat of tater tots and croissant sandwiches before they're ready to finish them. "Damn. Here she comes!" is always what I hear as I interrupt their parties and force them on their way.

"Okay, Ms. Riggs, we're hurrying! We're hurrying!"

"No one gets to college hangin' out in Burger King, folks! Get movin'!" is what I tell them.

Truancy is a challenge we continue to battle in an urban school located in the midst of a business district and in a school building where the doors can be easily pushed open for escape. We try many ways to combat the problem, and one of them is to simply go after our skippers. Many times, I have gone on cruiser rides with our school resource officer to round up kids who are supposed to be in school but instead are roaming the neighborhood. It is amazing, as we are literally flying down the alleys of the neighborhood in the cop car, bouncing over bumps in the pavement, observing as kids actually try to run from us. They run like scavengers, trying to avoid being caught. It's crazy. That's all right, though, because between the two of us, we can usually figure out the names of the runners and are able to follow up once back at school. The non-runners will concede to being caught and either follow my direction of, "You better get back to the building before I do," or they get into the cruiser for a personal escort to the front door. Hilarious scenes of gotcha!

One day, I roamed into the gym to watch the boys' basketball team during one of their after-school practices. I stood against the wall and took in the energy of their hard workout, watching sweaty boys go up and down the court and listened to the coaches as they directed their prepared drills. The team's manager, a very proud graduate of our school, was still faithful to his high school team and the role of manager that he held for many years and would keep as long as the team wanted him. Evan was a special education student, perhaps challenged in academic and social skills but advanced in his level of heart. He stood beside me filling water bottles and motivating his team with constant cheers.

"Good job, Bobby! Way to go, Tyler!" Constantly, Evan would blurt out cheers and the players were so obviously fond of him for his enthusiasm and were respectful of his limitations. Evan and I were among the few white faces in the gym, as all but one of our players on the team were African American.

Suddenly, my endearing facial expression at Evan's kudos to the players moved to one of mortification.

"Pick it up, Boy!" yelled Evan to one of our players.

"Evan! Honey, you can't call any of the players *Boy*!"

94

My heart jumped to imagine the negative reaction this last directive from Evan would surely create, and I knew I would have to further explain for some cultural proficiency to this young man why he should never call an African American boy "Boy."

The only reaction I got was when Evan corrected me and said, "But Ms. Riggs, his name is Boy!"

Indeed, the player's name was Boi.

# Chapter 15

## *ISMS* IN THE URBAN SCHOOLS

Respect. Big, bold, red letters that drape the main wall of the student commons area is what staff, students, and all guests to Omaha South view as they enter our school. A symbol, a mantra of our school family that so demonstratively surrounds us and so clearly is recognized in behaviors we witness, as either examples of, or examples of not. Stories of respect and dignity to each other are evident. Stories of disrespect are also recognized when observed as nonexamples. Some of each are observed by both adults and students, inside and outside of the school walls.

We celebrate courageous representations of respect. We damn those situations that clutter our school's vision when they reflect clear disrespect. Fighting is disrespectful. Kindness reflects respect. Respect must be reciprocal among staff and students. Prejudice of any kind violates all of the components of a respectful school. Sometimes it comes in a blatant form that becomes easy to stand up to and do the right thing in response to it. Sometimes, unfortunately, prejudice is less obvious and comes out less consciously, yet it's nonetheless important to watch out for and address.

Our kids are a reflection of our larger society and in a world where racism, sexism, classism, and prejudice against sexual orientation are still so ever present outside the school doors, we are negligent if not to recognize it within. I wish for a day in which I would not have as many examples as I do to write the chapter on isms as lengthy as it is, with new examples of it collected each and every day.

## Fighting the Prejudice of Sexual Orientation

"How dare you allow that club that promotes homosexual behavior into your school? My son goes to those meetings and those sponsors and those gay kids are going to try to make my son a faggot, too. He is *not* allowed to go to those meetings, Ms. Riggs, and I am holding you responsible if you let him attend."

"Faggot, Mrs. Johnson? If we're going to talk about this, please don't use that kind of language. The GSA Club is an after-school club that promotes respect of all students. The purpose is not to promote homosexuality but to allow our gay students and their straight friends a place where they can discuss ways to create safe atmospheres at school, where all students feel respected and safe. Many of the kids from the Christian Club also support the goals of GSA and attend those meetings as well. Alex is your son. If you don't want him attending, that is a decision that you and your family need to make. I will not force him to attend, nor will I force him not to attend."

I explained my stance with a little more attention to the subject than I needed to show her I would not engage in a debate with her beyond the existence of the club, as she truly wanted to do in the conversation. Her agenda was clearly to lecture me about the evil sins of homosexuality, as she put it. It irritated her greatly that I would not engage in the debate. She restrategized her efforts with an attempt to stir the issue by sending threatening e-mails about how she would put an end to this practice in the public schools, followed by other e-mails that lectured me about God. Some things don't warrant responses. Her e-mails did not. Our GSA club continues to meet after school and I believe that its sponsors are saving lives.

Sometimes the lesson of respect is challenged when our student body is faced with blatant prejudice and is expected not to retaliate with what they believe is justice. When the anti-gay group from the Westboro Baptist Church from Topeka, Kansas, announced to our city that they would be present at our school's dismissal one day, and at our graduation ceremony a few days later, it was tough to prepare our students to respond with dignity toward this group of hateful protesters. When our kids know something is wrong, they will do everything in their power to express it. We've taught them that—to speak out against social injustices and take stances. I squirmed, however, as I thought of the ways in which they might want to show their own protest toward this group, always having our school's reputation in the forefront as we fight false perceptions of who are kids are. I had to do everything in my power to make sure that the likely media attention would not shift from this group of crazy protesters to what appeared to be mobs of crazed South High students.

Our students were the target of this prejudice and the evil antics because the group follows school Web sites, watching schools with GSA groups and strategically plans their dramatic show, carrying signs that read, "God Hates Fags," and "Fag Enablers." They also picket at the funerals of military soldiers, contending that God punishes soldiers because the government has the "Don't Ask, Don't Tell" philosophy of allowing gay soldiers to fight in the military. Truthfully, however, their real agenda is money. The Phelps family, who leads the church and the protests, are mostly lawyers. Their tactic is to announce to cities that they will be present to execute their constitutional right of freedom of speech and are, therefore, guaranteed protection from potential anti-protesters who may get violent. They give exact dates, times from start to finish, and locations, expecting a specific area designated for their activity by the local authorities. They give clear notice of their presence and their intentions. They know the laws, inside and out. If something happens to them, they turn around and sue the city for not protecting them. This is how they financially survive, by preying on the vulnerabilities of grieving families and communities and clearly hoping that their messages incite a situation that may put them in danger.

Upon word of their upcoming visit, our kids blasted through Facebook, spreading the message that Westboro would be here, recruiting South High students and others across the district to be sure to show up in anti-protest. The upcoming scene took some very special teaching to our student body who couldn't believe what they were about to witness.

"Ms. Riggs, you would never let us do something like that! Why are they allowed to stand over there and say whatever they want?"

"Oh, no! We will not have them talking about our school like that!"

It became a real-life lesson in the US Constitution. Was this what our forefathers meant when they created the right to gather and speak freely? None of the textbooks that covered this important piece of American government described the possibilities of this group's presence. Did these great men really mean that people had the right to spew hatred and try to incite crowds? How could our kids express their own free speech against these hateful antics without appearing as out of control as the protesters? How do we make our students understand that ignoring them meant defeating them? To scream back, to throw rocks, and to do all of the natural reactions their hearts wanted to do would mean the protesters win. We want our students to think critically and debate what is right and wrong in order to have them contribute to the building of a strong society.

I envisioned with such trepidation the end-of-the-school-day bell ringing and a mad rush of students —some for the curiosity and some with a cause—rushing the doors to see the freak show of the Phelps family. To be a principal with that out-of-control feeling is the worst. The unknown outcome of what could mean mob mentality and danger was stressful to say the least. Had I prepared well enough for all of the possibilities?

I'd strategically placed staff in places around the building to do our best to minimize what could be a blast of negative energy. District officials were holding their assigned posts around the campus and in the direct vicinity of the protesters, ready to hold our students back if they charged. Police were visible as well. I was ready, too, walkie-talkie in hand, watching the time and balancing my emotions with the slow click of the second hand on my watch that would momentarily mean the dismissal bell and possible chaos.

In the midst of all the frightening anticipation, and the worry I tried so hard to hide, something truly amazing happened—something that no well-intended crisis planning would have ever insured me of. It was as if God himself said, "No worries, Cara. I've got this taken care of for you. I will handle these lost souls misrepresenting my Word." And without any warning, or any hope for the possibility, the rain came pouring down like torrential cats and dogs. It was so heavy and mixed with such strong winds, you could hardly see an arm's length in front of you, let alone make out the rancid letters that spelled the messages of abomination on the Topeka signs. No one, except a few diehard seniors and some of their radical, yet peaceful friends from GSA groups across the city were out with their own signs to protest the protesters. Christians from neighborhood churches, on the other hand, showed up in the pouring rain to spread love instead, water drenching their pant legs, even under their umbrellas. Students rushed from the building, indeed, but only to get on their busses with the least amount of damage to their soon-to-be soggy clothes. The only new reality of a fear of safety that had shrouded my head just moments prior to the rain, was the new worry of someone slipping in their sprint to their bus.

Divine intervention, indeed, was witnessed. We won in their game. They did not receive the attention they so hoped their trip to Omaha would create. The Westboro Baptist Church folks turned in defeat, signs smeared and sagging, tattered from the rain and wind, surrendering to God and the South High community, fighting to get to their cars through the storm and the wind.

Privately, however, even though I'd taught our students that ignoring the Phelpses was our best defense, I couldn't help myself when two of the Phelps daughters walked past me within inches of my reach. With a voice only they could hear, unable to fight the temptation, I said with direct eye contact, "You, should be ashamed of yourselves." And though I wasn't modeling what I'd taught my students to avoid, I must admit it felt good. Their showing up at graduation was just as nonproductive. And they went home, a wasted trip, only to target their next community, I'm sure.

They returned, however, a year later with another attempt to provoke our school community when they announced their intention to participate in the same kind of protest at the funeral of one of our beloved teachers who died suddenly when struck by a car.

Our school took on an enormous level of sadness at the tragedy of this loss, especially her students and colleagues. How dare they attempt, again, to provoke us with their antagonism and try to minimize her death? Through the tears and deep anguish, how could they be so evil to trespass on our pain? They called her a "Fag Enabler" and said her death was a direct punishment from God for the school's tolerance and acceptance of gay and lesbian students.

The community of Omaha was outraged and was determined to protect our students, staff, and the family of our teacher, Mrs. Stacy Klinger, by physically blocking the presence of this group from those who were grieving her loss and attending her funeral by overpowering in number, their presence. People came from all over the city to form a human chain that very peacefully barricaded the group's mission from even being seen. Three times, our school was forced to react to these antics and each time, did so with class and strength. This ism will continue to be a fight.

# With the Backdrop of Illegal Immigration Issues in the United States

Recruitment Open House is our school's opportunity to welcome perspective families looking for the high school that fits their needs as they make that choice from middle school to high school. Omaha South is known for its magnet programs in visual and performing arts, information technology, and dual language. The evening is rich with staff and students showing all of the programming available to a young person who might pick South as their high school home. All throughout the building, one can see students who are proud of their school and excited about the classes and activities they are involved in: the very best showmanship of all that there is to offer at our school. Everywhere our visitors turn, they can find excited and happy students who reflect the rich diversity of our school. Who wouldn't want their kid to go to this school?

"Are you the principal?" asked a woman standing there with a young girl I presumed to be her daughter.

"Yes. I'm Cara Riggs. Welcome to South High School, and your name?"

I put out my hand to show my sincere happiness to have them both here. No return of the gesture. No smile on her face, like I had on mine.

Just, "My daughter will *never* go to this school. We don't like Mexicans."

She turned on her heels, face scrunched with ugly, venomous eyebrows and wrinkles, daughter in tow with one hand pulling her by the sleeve, and walked down the hall to the front door, never to return. I froze in my shoes for a few seconds, mortified that anyone could have such thoughts, let alone say something like that out loud. Mortified but not really surprised. I shook my head and felt a sense of gratitude that the woman exposed her true colors upfront and would not be joining our school family.

"Is this the principal?" a caller asked from the other side of the line.

"Yes, this is Cara Riggs. Who am I speaking to?"

"Never mind what my name is. I just want to talk to you, because I just picked up my daughter for a doctor's appointment, and she told me something I just want make sure is not true. She said that during the morning bulletin read over the school's intercom system for everyone to hear, that the announcements were done in English and Spanish? Tell me that's not true."

"Actually," I said, "that is true. I believe we did have part of the bulletin read in Spanish this morning. What did you say your name was?"

"I told you to never mind what my name was. How dare you do anything in Spanish? Those Mexicans that come over here better learn English if they want to stay here. They come to our country then they better learn our language—blah, blah, blah—something about 90 percent of our students are probably illegal aliens—blah, blah, blah."

"Ma'am, I am not at all interested in talking to you about something so ridiculous, especially if you're not even brave enough to reveal who you are."

"Oh," she said, "so I suppose you're going to call me a racist now, too?"

"Yes, I am," I said without hesitation.

"Well, how dare you. I am going to call your superintendent and report you, and tell him that you are allowing announcements to be read in Spanish and . . . and . . . and that you had the nerve to call me a racist."

"May I save you the time and give you his phone number?" Click. She hung up.

Mrs. Klinger, our beloved social studies teacher, had just died after a tragic accident where she was hit by a car after school, walking to the parking lot. We were all dealing with the tragedy as best we could when I received the following voicemail: "Yeah. I just wanted to call and say I was sorry about what happened to your teacher over there. That's really too bad, but I'm not surprised. My daughter went to your school and it was terrible. I had to take her out of there. She got all involved with all those Mexicans at your school. Now she's at Boys Town and doing really well. Yeah, I just can't believe those Mexican gang members did something so terrible as to run your teacher over with their car, purposely. Yeah, if you want to talk to me about it, call me back at . . ."

What? Mexican gang members who purposely ran our teacher over with their car? Where in her wild imagination did she come up with that? No thanks. The last thing on earth I would do that day—or any day for that matter—would be to call this woman back.

Two students, one Hispanic, one African American. During an English class, the young men got into an argument that was disruptive and though it did not turn physical, required the teacher to intervene to insure it didn't. Both boys were sent to their administrators who mediated. Both boys agreed that they participated and contributed equally to the disruption. The boys were given the same consequence. After the parents were called and informed of the sequence of events, the mother of the African American student came up to appeal the decision with me, disagreeing that her son should have a consequence at all. She argued that the other boy started it and that her son had a right to defend himself, and it shouldn't matter that it happened because it didn't turn into a fight.

"Why is my son getting a consequence when he didn't even fight? So what if they argued. If that teacher had better control of his class, it never would have gone that far."

I held my ground with the decision to give the boys consequences.

Mom said, "Fine. I'm going to tell my son that the next time he should just smack the boy if he talks shit to you again. What's the difference if he's going to get a consequence, he might as well get a punch in. He is not going to that in-school suspension room. I'll just keep him home and you can suspend him out of school."

"Mrs. Smith, I'm not asking your permission to discipline Anthony. You and I will just have to agree to disagree on this one."

"Come on, let's get out of here," she said to Anthony and his uncle who had come to support Mom. "I can see that the Mexicans run the school around here, not you," she said as she stormed out the door, uncle right behind her and Anthony grinning at me as if to say, "See. Don't mess with me. My mom always sticks up for me."

"USA! USA!" shouted a crowd of all-white male students from the local private boy's high school when they waited to play the basketball game after ours at the State Basketball Tournament.

Tortillas thrown on the court during a volleyball game.

Sombrero's worn by some of the home team fans at an away football game.

A small town in Nebraska hosts a district basketball game where our team travels to play. All but one of our players is African American. The all-white opposing team includes a kid in the student section of student fans, dressed in a gorilla suit. And when we addressed the issue with the administration of the school? "Oh, it was just a joke."

Another small town in Nebraska where our school's very diverse show choir travels to compete in a vocal music competition. Our kids exit the bus along the main strip and separate in small groups to eat at the various fast food restaurants during their quick break. One young man chooses a restaurant to enter by himself. The joint was filled with white people; he's the only African American there. Heads turned, whispers were rampant, and a young mother even scurried her young children as if to say they weren't safe with the boy's entrance into the establishment. Our student began to feel unsafe. Especially when two white police officers entered the restaurant and checked him out, up and down with a look like he didn't belong. How ironic: officers of the law, supposed to represent safety, security and comfort, exactly the opposite. Our student's paranoia? His overreaction? I doubt it. He left, with not one person making him feel welcome to be a visitor in that town.

After playing their first football game in our school's brand new stadium, some of our football players, all geared up in our school sportswear, went to a local restaurant to celebrate their win, the amazing show of school pride from the community, and making history as the first team in the school's archives to play in this million-dollar facility. They filled their plates from the buffet and all sat together in celebration to fellowship with one another. The table was a beautiful mix of black, white, and Hispanic players. Within moments of their late night dinner, before any of them even thought about the dessert line, a man approached their table and got the attention of the team with, "You all play for South?" The boys affirmed the question with pride and delight, all assuming the stranger was surely interrupting to give them a congratulations or some other compliment.

"What a waste. All that taxpayer money spent on that new stadium for you all? Huh."

The boys got restless and immediately agitated, probably moments from all standing up to give the drunk a piece of their minds in great harmony. One of the players, however, a senior, took lead and stood up, calming his teammates with his voice, demeanor, and arm gestures and said, "Never mind, fellas. It's not worth it. Look man, we're just sittin' here minding our own business."

The drunk's tablemate tried to pull him away from the boys, realizing his level of rudeness, hopefully embarrassed and probably worried about an ugly outcome. Finally, the manager came over and insisted that the drunk leave the restaurant. He did, not very willingly, and not without the threat of calling the police. I received a call the next Monday from a patron at another table who witnessed the entire event. He told me how proud I could be of the South High football players for their class and strength in the face of adversity. I was indeed.

Graduation night, 2010: 320 seniors and their friends and family, celebrating the academic milestone of the finish of high school; balloons, flashing cameras, air horns, hugs, and flowers. It was a double celebration with Omaha South High Magnet School's State Championship Soccer game immediately following the graduation ceremony. A sea of red caps and gowns and thousands of fans from the entire city could be seen entering the stadium to witness the final game of the tournament. Who will be the champion and earn the trophy? The stadium was filled with fans that matched the demographics of their schools. From Lincoln, fans from the suburban high school as excited about the chance to win as the fans from Omaha, in full cheer for the urban school. Other Omaha fans, whose teams did not make it to the final, also crowded the stands in support of our school. "If our team can't win it, we want yours to," was the local sentiment.

The stadium was packed to the brim with every seat filled and fans seated along the hill on both end zones. It was truly the best two teams in the state playing hard against each other, both equally as talented, and both equally wanting that title.

The game went into overtime. The crowd was wild with that same championship energy that can be felt at the Super Bowl, or the World Cup, or an NBA Final game. Both teams were about to be winners, no matter what the outcome would be, but only one would take home the trophy.

"May the best team win," was what it all came down to. With a pins and needles shootout, South lost by one goal. And with the blow of the horn came the screams from both crowds and a mad rush of the fans from the winning school, down to the field. Our fans were busy trying to absorb the reality that we'd lost and comfort each other in the letdown, deflated from full energy and enthusiasm to a sudden and drastic letdown.

All of a sudden, from the side of the eye, one could see tons of what looked like green confetti fly up from a section of the crowd that had rushed the field. Confetti? A planned gesture of celebration, if they won? Soon, however, it began to be clearer about the intention and message of the gesture. True symbolism. Soccer is a game of penalties with yellow and red cards thrown by referees to symbolize violations. This gesture? Green cards thrown to express anti-illegal immigration sentiments to our largely Hispanic community and our almost 100 percent Hispanic team. There was local and national news coverage for two weeks straight—outrage and anger—hurt and sadness—shock in reading editorials with ignorant responses to the situations. Our kids were worn down by the attention.

"Can't we just stop talking about it?" they'd say. The media hounded us. The two schools wanted to grow from what happened. A secret breakfast meeting arranged by the two principals included ten students from each school to share feelings and plan for what to do next. Their goals were to use the situation to grow. They wanted their two student bodies to better understand each other, admitting that their two school communities were so different and that ignorance comes from not knowing and not understanding each other. The incident brought about feelings of disrespect and shame. Their kids had to express their embarrassment for their peers who participated. Our kids had to express their hurt for the act of prejudice.

"We're so sorry this happened."

"This happens to us more than you'd know."

Healing and forgiveness would play on for months and months in response. Two school communities were able to build bridges through better understanding of each other's cultures with the student exchanges initiated by the two schools. Real friendships were started. Facebook friends and groups from each school showed up to support the others at their own sporting events. Sometimes good things come from bad incidents. This was one of them. We only hope the adults learned as much as the kids did. We don't know what we don't know.

"Aren't you afraid down there, with those kids?" Often a question I get when I reveal that I am the principal of South High. Down there. Those kids. They are shocked when I respond that I love being in that community with our students. "Really?" Yes. Really.

One of our visual arts majors entered one of her paintings into the Congressional Art Contest hosted by our US congressman The student was notified that she was the winner and was given a beautiful letter of congratulations. The piece would be matted and framed and she and her mother would be flown to Washington, DC, where the piece would be hung for special recognition. The day of the local ceremony, when representatives from the congressman's office evidently looked closer at the piece, they realized the work reflected a message of the fears of border control in this country.

A call to the student's teacher by someone representing the congressman's office indicated that they had "changed their mind," that the piece was "too controversial," but that we could choose one of her other works to be displayed because "she did deserve to win ... just not with that particular piece." I quickly e-mailed the congressman and asked how he suggested I explain this unbelievable decision to this student. No answer. Our student and her mother declined the congressman's offer and the second-place winner moved to first place and received the award, the trip to Washington, and the display. It was a horrible example—or perhaps, a perfect example—of how our government sometimes works. I was proud of the decision that Laura made to reject the offer of avoiding controversy.

## Not All Celebrate One God

"I'm calling to follow up on a complaint to verify if it is true that your school has a 'Muslim chapel,'" said a representative from the ACLU. This was one of many calls I received from some Omaha citizens and in follow up by district officials who were also receiving complaints. No. Not a "Muslim chapel." We do, however, accommodate a few Muslim students who wish to pray privately during their lunchtime by providing actually one of two places: a closet, curtained off in the nurse's office or in my private bathroom. There are no organized religious ceremonies with incense and beads, just out of the way locations that do not disrupt instruction or anyone else's educational experience.

"And is it true that you deny the same accommodation to your Christian and Jewish students when they ask?" No. Not true.

Once again, more evidence of prejudice and disrespect, under the guise of Jesus.

# Chapter 16

## A STORY OF TOUGH LOVE

Sometimes the actions in love stories take on a different form. Sometimes one must play tough love with one family member to protect and show love for the larger family.

The bell had rung for first period to begin. The few students left in the hallway were stragglers being told to hustle, as they were now tardy. Teachers were in their classrooms beginning their lessons, like any other morning, like any other Wednesday. Just a few of us remained outside the main office at the entrance corridor, still drinking our coffee, and happy to begin the hump day with half of the week almost behind us.

Monday and Tuesday had been rainy, which always seemed to create a fog of dark spirits, but today brought sunshine and the feeling that perhaps spring was truly on the way. Students and staff always appeared better geared up for the day when the sun was shining. Spirits were more pleasant with the heat of sun on their faces. Bus stops without rain meant no umbrellas. Car rides were smoother with a less dangerous feeling on the interstate ride in—a feeling of hope for springtime and flowers, good coffee with real cream, kids with smiles and positive energy anxious to see each other.

"Break that up over there. No one wants to watch that," I said to a couple embracing like young lovers, not caring who saw them kissing. "Take that hat off, or it's mine," I called out to Enrique, and then Marcus, and then Bobby, and about six others who seemed to always need reminders about our no-hat rule.

"Congratulations, Miss Qualls. You really cleaned up last night!" I said to a student who was so proud of herself at the JROTC awards ceremony the night before.

"Ladies, ladies! Volume, please. You're way too loud."

"Okay, Ms. Riggs, my bad!" said one of them.

"Leadership, gentlemen, leadership! Let's get moving and ready to get the day started."

"Nice hairdo, Erica! You look beautiful, girl" I said to Erica who obviously had been to the hairdresser since yesterday's pulled-back ponytail.

Typical morning conversations as kids get off their busses and wait for the first bell to ring. What a beautiful day. What a blessing to work here. And with a turn of my head, my life flashed before me. As quickly as the bell rang and those calm thoughts of victory for a smooth opening of the school day had run through my mind, my heart felt like it had stopped. I thought about my beautiful daughter who was somewhere in the building. Was she safe? Who would tell her about what had happened? My feet moved instinctively toward what looked to be horror unfolding. I didn't run. I didn't yell for help. No time. I simply moved toward what I feared to be disaster about to implode, as it was my responsibility to stop whatever was about to happen in our school.

Halfway down the hallway, I rushed toward a scene that seemed to move in slow motion. Darkness. A nightmare in action. He was dressed in black, from head to toe, like the villain in a superhero movie. He moved from around the corner at the end of the hall with a dark stocking cap wrapping his head and his face covered with a mask that only revealed his eyes and forehead. It looked like the mask of Hannibal Lector.

A nightmare. He lurked with his body bent slightly and his arms apart, one in front of the other, and wide enough apart that it made my eyes believe the figure was holding something the length of a rifle. Could that monster of darkness be springing down the school's hallway with a rifle, dressed in that stereotypical scary garb that prefaced clearly to me what would momentarily be another school shooting? A moment's flash. And that was what I feared was about to happen.

I must have yelled, "Hey! What the hell are you doing?" and in hindsight, putting myself in front of what so clearly looked like a perpetrator, and me as the first of his targets. Instead, the mask came off his face and there was clearly no rifle in those arms he used to reach toward his head to reveal his identity.

It was Jake. I knew Jake, and I ordered him to my office with every bit of anger and directness I'd ever felt myself exhibit.

"Give me that!" I said and snatched the mask from his hand as he cooperated and walked with me to my office. With the mistaken shooter, the shooter I had so vividly imagined in my head, I closed the door to my office.

Behind closed doors, I lost all semblance of professionalism that I'd forever been an expert in. Words unheard of in my vocabulary when dealing with kids appeared mysteriously from the depth of my soul in natural symphony, as if I used them on a daily basis.

"Shut your mouth! How could you be so stupid? What the hell were you thinking? Are you crazy?" These words—words that would cause me to go crazy on any other staff member who used them with our kids—came from my mouth.

I paced back and forth, not sure what I would do next. I didn't know myself. I knew, though, that my heart was pumping with such force and my body temperature had gone up so high I was sure I was close to a heart attack. No matter what I said, not the example of an airport scare, not the vision of what may have happened had a squad of police officers been in eyeshot, and not the intensity of my seriousness kept him from an explanation any better than, "I was just trying to make my friends laugh with my Ninja stuff. It was just a joke. I'm sorry."

Sorry wasn't good enough. The dean of students took Jake to his office. I had to regroup and pull myself together. I had to try to look at the situation with some kind of reason.

I wondered if I'd overreacted. Was I too emotional, exposing some obvious underlying fears I'd hidden in regard to years of hearing about school shootings? One was recent and local, where an assistant principal was shot and killed in her office and the principal critically wounded by a bullet in a rampage by a student who then took his own life. I needed to view the videotapes to see again what had unfolded. Was Jake a threat to the safety of our student body, or was I overly emotional?

I viewed the tapes with an assistant principal. The replay was as frightening to him as the original was to me. Memories of Columbine were strewn across the screen as if it happened yesterday. Still photos reminded us of the years of national coverage and pictures of Eric Harris and Dylan Klebold, the infamous shooters in the Columbine massacre. They looked like Jake. Dark. Villainous.

No, I had not overreacted. With the safety of our school always on my mind, this was one more reminder of the importance of vigilance in observation and supervision—always something new to debrief about. How would we handle things differently?

Were we lucky this time? Jake would have to go. Awakening. This could have been the real thing. It really could happen anywhere. What do I know for sure? I'll continue to ask God, every morning, to watch over our school and keep us safe.

# Chapter 17

## THE TRANSFORMATION OF DANIEL, A MAN OF HONOR

Hope. It evolves through our life experiences and is torn down quickly through a change in circumstances. Hope diminishes our faith in the world so suddenly, back to hopelessness. Hope to hopelessness will yank at the heart and will change the level of our motivation in life like the most dramatic of roller coaster rides. At the top of the ride, you are a believer, safe and confident that what you desire will occur. With the shift of the open car, the train winds down the track and flies over the trestle into the sharpest of inclines, plunging us to that state of a nonbeliever. From hope to hopelessness and waiting for signs to believe again: this is Daniel.

Daniel is no different than many young men in our school, but his story takes some twists that make him stand out as an extraordinary example of hope. It is truly a love story.

Daniel has a mom who loves him. She has raised him with the best of intentions that he and his siblings get the most out of life. But her best of circumstances has been tattered with realities of financial challenges that place limits on what the best will look like.

Survival was more like it. Low income forced Daniel's mom to move from home to home, from bad neighborhood to bad neighborhood. Bad neighborhoods equaled run-down homes with gang activity, dangerous to a mother trying to raise young boys and keep them away from the turf wars and lure of involvement. Daniel was not immune to that involvement, nor were his brothers. School was his only hope—and basketball— and Audrey.

Daniel was a fifth-year senior. His circumstances outside of school led to credit challenges and a deferred graduation. The relationship with his basketball coach and his teammates saved Daniel from giving up and dropping out of school. An appeal to the state's activities association allowed Daniel to benefit from an extra year of eligibility. Clearly, Daniel's basketball skills were good but not great, and an extra year of playing ball was more for him than for the team and its winning record; the team would have won with or without his membership. Daniel would not have won in life, however, without the team and the school's love. The school's dedication to Daniel and his success took him from being a once disrespectful and confrontational young man with his teachers, to a trusting and grateful kid who showed thanks and appreciation to our staff. The more he began to trust, the more great things seemed to come his way.

Audrey was Daniel's high school sweetheart. Rarely in today's school setting do we see that old-fashioned relationship of sweetheart that many of our moms and dads experienced at their young age—that she's my one and only, that loyalty of true blue, young love. Instead, we see so often our young people jump from relationship to relationship. They usually have no intention of staying with one in friendship and caring. At other times, we see kids sure that each one, time after time, is the one, only to be heartbroken once again.

Audrey and Daniel were true to each other and everyone believed they would forever be a couple. Audrey graduated before Daniel and the two still remained together, with Audrey attending college but always in attendance at Daniel's basketball games his senior year, supporting her high school boyfriend. Daniel admired and respected his Audrey and bragged about his college girl and how proud he was of her. Audrey was indeed stability for Daniel.

Stability wavered for Daniel. His basketball coach, his teachers, and our school administrators continued to provide Daniel with whatever support at school it took to keep him focused and believing in a hopeful future. We made sure he attended his senior prom when he thought he didn't need to have that memory. Handsome in his white tuxedo with a fresh haircut and his beautiful Audrey in a dress that matched his tie, Daniel walked into the party like he was eight feet tall, his girl on his arm. He was so happy and excited that he made it to his prom, taking pictures all night, posting them on his Facebook page for everyone to see. Daniel was stable and hopeful that night. This was what the best of school memories with your favorite girl was supposed to bring a child with hope.

The following Monday, Daniel's assistant principal called me to her office for some help with what was about to happen. She had received a call that Daniel's brother had just been shot at a convenience store across town and, like the cousin he walked in with, may not make it. We had to tell Daniel. The roller coaster was about to take the steep plunge of the ride. We prepared for the very worst of reactions and we were right.

Daniel walked into the office with a smile and a swagger, his arms spread out full length like he was going to get to hang out with two of the women he had grown to love and care for instead of be in class.

"What's up, ladies?" joked Daniel with every demeanor of respectful affection he so often showed. "Did you both call me down here?" he said with a huge smile on his face, quickly plopping in an office chair and getting comfortable as if to relax in someone's living room. He must have read immediately the tone of the visit was not one of play, as our faces read of somber and seriousness.

"Daniel."

"What's wrong?" and he shifted his body from the back of the chair to the front, with his elbows on his knees.

"Daniel. We just took a call that your brother was shot."

Daniel's jump from the chair was just how he'd leap when the coach called him off the bench and into the game, with the same speed, height, and urgency. He screamed and cried and swore revenge to whoever was responsible. His arms waved, starting with both hands on his head and then spreading out fully with his head tilted to the sky.

"Give me a phone. Give me a phone. Motha Fucka's gonna get theirs. Give me a phone," he yelled with volume increasing with each demand. He went within a millisecond from happy and hopeful to furious and committed to avenge what someone had done to his brother. Just that fast. Nothing else was important. Not school. Not his girl. Not his future.

His call was to what he knew the best and who he cared for the most: family—a cousin. The conversation revealed clearly to the two of us listening that the other person on the phone was in sync with Daniel's plan to "find out who did this," and that they'd "get theirs."

We gave Daniel a ride to the hospital. I don't think he heard a word we said the whole ride there, planning and plotting privately with his body moving from front to back of the school van's seat.

He jumped out of the vehicle and ran to his family, without a good-bye or a thank you or anything, probably with no memory of how he even got there or who even took him. All he cared about was his pledge to find the shooter.

We didn't see Daniel for another week. We couldn't find him, even when we looked at the hospital. We called his home. We called his cell phone. Nothing. He'd disappeared from anything but revenge.

We feared the worst, but hoped and prayed he wouldn't do what he had promised and that he would stay safe and be smart. I could not imagine how he was feeling, but I tried—and prayed.

We were so relieved when he came back to school and seemed less emotional and more rational. Daniel's brother would survive, but his condition was very serious and would result in months of rehabilitation. The shooter is still unknown.

Daniel's school support system rallied around Daniel with coaching on how much he would lose if he chose to pursue the retaliation he was so tempted with. It was tough. We had to listen and try to understand with the deepest of sensitivity what it meant to him to be tackling these feelings of retaliation as if there was no choice, no other way, no discussion.

We just didn't understand his logic, coming from our worlds. His world meant, "take care of it ourselves, 'cause the cops sure won't." We listened and coached and listened some more and recoached, over and over again, new adult after new adult, all going through the same process. He finally came around, we thought. We were not positive, but it appeared that Daniel again became hopeful about his future and we did not have any evidence he had done anything we had feared. (I am not naïve to believe the story would possibly have very been different had Daniel's brother died.)

One day, Daniel went to his assistant principal and asked her to put the following letter of thanks online to our school staff:

Dear Staff,

To all the staff who prayed for me, my brother and my family, I greatly appreciate you taking the time to put me and my family in your prayers, even though I'm nothing more than a student. It means a lot to me to know that you care that much to even think about me like that, not just a student, but someone who needed guidance at the time. Ms. Riggs, Mrs. Johnson, Mr. Huff, and Dr. Huerta comforted me the most the day tragedy hit me and my family hard. I thought I had lost my brother, but Ms. Riggs stayed with me the whole time and let me know that it was going to be all right. I lost my cousin that day, but I gained the comfort, love, and respect of other people that I never would have thought cared. I thought all teachers had to do was teach, not care or anything else, just teach and make rules, but that's not the case. Teachers at South High care a lot even if you're not the best kid. Mrs. Johnson and Dr. Huerta called me on my cell phone to check on me and my brother. At that moment, I felt the warmness in my heart. Honestly, I was surprised, but they really care and that means a lot. Mr. Huff got me home and he told me not to worry, everything was going to be all right, but at the same time he let me know that he was sorry for what happened. You all are very beautiful people and I appreciate the love and the caring that you gave me on my day of grief. So I just wanted to say thank you to all who prayed, the ones that were there and the ones who never left my side. Thank You Very Much.

Sincerely,
Daniel Mason

We were so shocked. And so pleased. You just never know if you are reaching a kid or not. Daniel's sentiments of gratitude were so powerful to all of us, validating to us why we come to work every day. Even teachers who did not know Daniel were inquisitive about who this sensitive and thoughtful young man was who sent such a note to us all.

Stability appeared to waver again, when Audrey became pregnant. Daniel was happy. He spoke of being the kind of daddy he never knew, the kind he had only dreamed about having, as his daddy was absent.

"Don't worry," he said. "We're not like everybody else. We'll be fine."

We were not happy with the reality of the two of them becoming parents; however, we continued to show Daniel support and guidance, and there was something in the two of them that made us believe if any two young people could tackle this, they could. The two were determined to be good parents and were clear about their plans to be a family, forever.

Daniel graduated from high school and enlisted in the Army. He was focused, excited, and had a clear vision of success in the future for him and his family. Daniel went off to boot camp and returned to visit us at school. I remember vividly the reaction of the adults who watched this tall gentleman enter the building. He was the soldier with the crisply ironed uniform, tall and lean, strong and proud, with the precision of a military man. He had a walk to him he didn't have before. It was that march that soldiers move with, straight and disciplined, serious and determined.

Teachers who knew him flocked to his side after a double take, realizing it was our Daniel. I watched as he received the exact reaction he hoped for as he returned to his school family: validation.

"Look at you!"

"Congratulations, young man."

"Daniel, you look so grown up!"

We were proud and confident in his purpose to provide his new wife and baby with a successful and happy future.

"You're really doin' it, Daniel," I whispered in his ear as I hugged him with faith and confidence and reassurance.

His next visit came with his baby son. This time he wanted us to see him as not only a soldier, but a father and a husband now—a daddy who loved his little boy. That he was: a soldier who would protect his country, a husband and father who would provide for his family. Transformation. A man of honor. Hope accomplished.

# Chapter 18

# THE POWER OF ACCESS

And then there was Anthony. Same school. A senior, afforded the same programming opportunities that everyone else in the school has been offered. The same teachers and counselors. A diverse set of friends that live in the same area of the city, urban Omaha. So why is his story of hope so different? And why are his hurdles so few? A love story, like the others, no doubt. Anthony was easy to love. Self-motivated. Never any challenges in behavior or difficulties with academics. The difference in Anthony's story? Access and the power of it.

Anthony is the kid that if perfection was real, and we know that no one is perfect, he is darn close. There really isn't anything that I found negative about him, not that I'm searching. In fact, my daughter and I joke that Anthony is her future husband. He's the kind of kid that you hope your daughter falls in love with and marries someday, surely living happily ever after. He's the full package of character, intelligence, well-roundedness, sense of humor, drive, focus, and so much more. He's been the high-achieving student with the leadership qualities that have involved him in many positions both inside and outside of school. He's the kid with a job and the kid that always volunteers his time, as well. Anthony is a role model that all other students look up to, the one who is so gregarious that he is respected by not only other high-achieving and high-functioning students and all of our staff, but also by our more challenged students who may even be in trouble. There have been no haters, wishing he'd fail. How could that be? He's not selfish. Probably because he prides himself on being kind to all people and in taking the time to show interest and attention to the lives of all around him. If he sounds like a future president of the United States, one who could really rescue the country, he could be, with no surprise to anyone. People just want to be around him and watch how he functions. Anthony's success and clear pathway of a hopeful future comes from the access created by his family.

Access does not necessarily mean money. Anthony is a member of a very humble family, well respected in the community, which has birthed generations of college graduates. They're not rich. They work hard. His parents and sisters, aunts, uncles, and cousins, however, are all products of post-secondary education. He grew up seeing, hearing, and knowing that it was never a question of whether or not he'd go to college, but only where he'd attend and what he'd study. Education has been the expectation, not the dream. His access has also included the value systems that mirror success in all areas of life.

There is monumental pride in Anthony's Hispanic heritage and in the culture of his Hispanic community. His family values community, the responsibility of service, and giving back to those who have worked hard before you. Anthony walks and talks the value of respect to all people and his relationships, as a result, are positive and healthy and attract others with like mission and purpose. His family radiates with what is right and good in people, and that the more you give in life, the more you get back. Anthony's family has modeled much success in their careers in the local community, with honored advancements in their various fields. This access to purposeful values of greatness has afforded Anthony with the ethic of hard work that led him to amazing opportunities as he exited high school and entered college. His many scholarships and honors for his academic success and leadership had been the rewards of all of the years of access to those values.

It was no surprise that the student chosen to speak at graduation was Anthony. He's been the easy kid to educate and among the greatest of ambassadors of our school. Access has been the difference between Anthony and so many of his peers.

So how does a school begin to make up for the lack of access that so many of our students, unlike Anthony, have been dealt? Providing opportunities and experiences that students cannot get on their own can boost our students' level of hope and belief in their own possibilities.

At our school, we are blessed with a philanthropic community that has done amazing things to provide access to students that they would not otherwise be able to experience. With the Warren Buffett family right here in our backyard, all staunch believers in the power of an outstanding public school system and the effects that it has on the future of our community and our country, their foundations have provided enormous dollars that allow us to actualize hope in our students.

Another initiative that has brought huge dollars to public school students in our community is the Building Bright Futures organization, also a result of community leaders and donors who understand that the schools alone cannot be responsible for the future of our kids, and the more the community invests in their futures, the more we will all benefit down the road. None of us in Omaha take for granted these incredibly generous contributions that we know do not exist in most other cities. Though dollars are nice and we have enormous gratitude to these donors, the investment from people of their sincere time and energy spent with our students is the most powerful dividend.

The process of applying for college scholarships is an example of access that many students without the level of parental involvement and investment of time that Anthony has, will never tackle, as it is extremely intimidating and complicated. Only the truly determined and those given a great deal of hand-holding get through the process from start to finish. The hand-holding is important, and it's vital that a school has a team of people focused to assist students every step of the way. Beginning as early as possible, it is a responsibility of our staff to weed through all of the common hopeless comments we hear from kids like, "I can't ever go to college," "No one in my family has ever gone to college, so I won't be able to go either," "I'm not smart enough to go to college," "I've been in too much trouble to go to college," or "I just hope I'll graduate from high school; college wasn't even in my plans."

These statements of nonbelievers, always from those without access like Anthony, are rampant in urban schools. Many kids have not even been on a college campus, so it is our job to round up our kids and get them on organized visits to campuses and give them the opportunity to see themselves there and to see other college students who look like them being successful in a post-secondary school experience.

The Susan Thompson Buffett Foundation, one of the Warren Buffett family foundations, offers many scholarship opportunities to students in our community who are first-generation, college-bound kids. Our school's seniors have received over 100 of these full-ride scholarships in the past two years. This is amazing, but we clearly know that without the focused assistance, motivation, encouragement, and follow-through of school staff, those numbers would not be as high at our school. It's not about putting a bulletin announcement over the PA system that says, "Pick up the Buffett Scholarship Application in the counseling center if you are interested in applying." It just wouldn't happen without focused steps like opening up the computer lab for students applying for particular scholarships to gather to write their essays with adult guidance. Or clear instruction of the process of filling out FAFSA (Free Application for Federal Student Aid) forms and other purposeful hand-holding steps. We must provide access to students who do not have it.

Social access is not only limited in schools where there is high poverty, but practically nonexistent unless we provide it.

What our students have been exposed to socially does not compare to what their counterparts in the suburban and private schools have seen and experienced. Access to culture, like music, theater, travel, and so many other experiences that typically equate to what the haves and have-nots know, so deeply affects the level of hope that students have for their futures that most people who are haves would be shocked to understand.

*West Side Story,* a classic, award-winning Broadway production, should be something that all kids get to experience. At our school, with 60 percent of our student body Hispanic, no one had ever seen the famous show and many had never even heard of it. How could that be? So when the production came to Omaha on the big stage, we found funding to allow several busloads of our students access to this theatrical experience. Our kids were in awe and so outwardly moved by the performance and the storyline that mirrored many of their own lives, that it was beautiful to witness. Most of our students had not been to any theater production outside of our school performances. This was their very first time.

First times are common for many of the outings and simple experiences we provide our students. One of our Sudanese students asked if he could earn some extra money, and I told him I had some yard work he could do over the weekend. He drove to my home and immediately rang the doorbell and began to look around like my house was the biggest and fanciest thing he'd ever seen. He was complimentary about how beautiful he thought it was, with eyes open wide, head slowly scoping the view from the living room to the dining room, and up the staircase and said, "Do you and your daughter really live in this big place alone?" I noticed how he gazed at the art on the walls, the rugs on the floor, and the knickknacks, details he wasn't familiar with. The two of us went to get flowers and mulch so he could get my spring yard spruced up and planting of potted flowers done for the season. We also put an empty propane tank for my gas grill in my trunk so that I could get it refilled.

From start to finish with those common things in my day-to-day life, nothing that I would consider extravagant, this young man had no familiarity with any of it.

"So what is this mulch stuff for, Ms. Riggs?" Just like a blind person who recently regains his sight, I had to explain, show, and model the use of and process of spreading what I have known to be a staple in pretty yards my whole life, something this young man had never known in his. This student was fascinated and said, "We just don't see mulch in the projects where I live, and we never saw it in Sudan, Ms. Riggs. It's cool, though. I'll be looking around and noticing it when I drive now. You learn something new every day, huh?"

The planting of beautiful flowers in pots around the outside of the house brought about the same kind of curiosity and inquisition for this young man. The concept of a gas grill and how the propane tank provided an easy flame to quickly and conveniently grill burgers and steaks was also foreign to him. He said, "We just throw burgers in the skillet and fry 'em up on the stove in my house. This is cool how this works. I want one of these!" I would nearly die without my gas grill and he now views it as something he aspires to have in his own home—someday. There is so much we take for granted and so much we can't even fathom that our students do not have a clue of.

When gas grills and potted flowers are new to our kids, think about the larger things in life they have no concept of except for what they see on television. High paying jobs, fine homes, and travel to beautiful places are things that other people get to experience, not them. These are things so far from their belief of what is reachable that it becomes one of our biggest challenges in schools to make them believers, that they too can have those things in their own futures. The clichés of "You can be whatever you want to be" or "You can do whatever you want to do in life" are not seen as truthful statements to most urban kids. They believe, like many of their family members believe, that they will need to keep buying lottery tickets for any possibility of having those things—like it's all about luck.

"Yeah, right, Ms. Riggs. You're rich. I'm not. I'll never have that."

Even their concept of rich is amazing. I am certainly not close to being rich, but to kids who don't have much and who only dream of fine things and see them as unattainable, rich is not very rich. So when we take groups of kids to local fundraising dinners that are $75 a plate, they are wowed. Beef tenderloin with garlic mashed potatoes and fresh asparagus, a Caesar salad, and a *crème brûlée* for dessert are almost frightening to these kids.

With each new food item, they look to you with that polite but fearful face that reads, "Oh, no. I don't know what this is, Ms. Riggs. Help me." I politely move my body closer to them so that I can whisper what it is, assure them they should trust that it is delicious, and not embarrass them for their ignorance of what they don't know. We don't know what we don't know.

I watch as they fiddle with their forks, inspecting each bite of meat, flipping and flopping it over and over, some never taking the risk of it being something they won't like. Are they sneaking bites under the table to a puppy I'm unaware of like the way I once fooled my own mom when she served corned beef? Others, so used to the routine of beef, potatoes, and corn, brave the new cuisine and look over to report with their faces whether they like it or not. Either heads nod and a second and third bite shows their approval, or that, "I don't think I can swallow this so what should I do with it now" look reveals their disappointment and defeat and desperation to be saved, without anyone but me knowing they hate it.

Some of them, however, say they don't even want to attend the event when we reveal that they have to dress up. We know immediately what that really translates to is, "I don't have anything to wear." No problem. We have a "career closet" at school that can privately take care of that problem for kids and not leave them out of experiencing new social events and keynote speakers that they will enjoy being a part of and hopefully be inspired by. It's filled with donations of beautiful suit jackets, white shirts, ties, dress pants, and business suits. They need to be able to see themselves in those situations to believe they can be a part of them on their own, in their adult futures. We need to provide them these opportunities or they may never have another chance.

Being dressed to the nines like everyone else in the room of this high-ticket fundraising event convinces them that they, too, can fit in. It's that young man who has never had a crisply ironed white shirt and a cool tie under a jacket that, though, it's a hand-me-down, nobody knows because it looks brand new. It's as if he walked out of the dressing room at Saks Fifth Avenue. He's sharp. He's proud. He's confident. Just like the rich guys in the room that indeed may have purchased theirs at Saks. I read their minds, "Look at me. I am somebody, too. See Armani on this label? Guess what kind of car I drove up in? Yeah, the valet parked my black Mercedes. Guess which neighborhood I live in? It's me. Believe it. Watch me. I'll be there and I'm going to prove it to you." All while he grips his tie and straightens his shoulders, walking a little taller. Access. That's what it does.

Dance lessons, private piano and tennis instruction, club swimming, and private tutors are all realities for kids with access because their parents can afford them. They are common to rich kids, likely participating in multiple activities that cost parents big dollars, whose parents don't blink an eye at paying for them. Access to these privileges sets these lucky students well ahead in every game they want to play, in sports, in the arts, and academically. Accessed kids are far ahead of our students when they have had the privileges they are so accustomed to, and likely even take for granted. Privileged students don't even understand the concept of access until it's explained to them.

As a school, we want to provide exposure for the first time. We find funds to have professional dance teachers instruct our dance program. We provide the same experts that, outside of school, have been teaching privileged kids, year after year, with specialized class after specialized class, and recital after recital for hundreds and hundreds of dollars per dancer over those young lives. Real ballet slippers and tap shoes, costumes and recitals are what our kids get from their school experience, like other kids get with outside studio lessons. I watch these young women run from one tutu to another, smiling and proud of what must feel like a scene from the movie *Fame*. This is their performing arts school; it's their performing arts experience that will hopefully provide them a level of new confidence and feeling of beauty, grace, and elegance that they would not have had without us. Our auditorium is packed at our dance recital, as these families are first timers to how elaborate this event is, with their child likely dancing in two or three dances each. Moms and dads bring bouquets of flowers for their first-time ballerinas, just as if they were performing on a New York City stage. Wild applause and cheers for every single routine that includes thirty-forty kids per dance, bounces off the walls of the standing-room-only event. It's no less an event than the privileged kids have, whose parents pay big dollars for their lessons and their end of the year recital.

"Mija, tu eres Hermosa . . . Hermosa."

The proud papa, with tears in his eyes, hugs his little ballerina as if she's three years old again, perhaps the time that most little girls with access and affluence get to start with their lessons.

"Mija, tu eres Hermosa."

Priceless. We've created exposure and access.

We have also created a dynamic and exclusive public school piano program that has thirty piano stations. Students take piano for credit and move from one level to the next, with four years of daily lessons. Imagine what forty minutes a day, five days a week, nine months a year for four years can bring to a student who is serious about learning piano. Even if they don't have a piano at home that they can practice on, and almost none do, they have an opportunity to go from a beginner to proficient with four years of private teaching. It's been an extraordinary experience to watch the growth of students who walked in never touching the keys and who leave our school with a lifelong skill in piano. The piano lab is packed each period and has gone from one part-time teacher to two working full time.

Richard is from Burma. He's ready for Julliard. No kidding. His body moves from side to side with the same cadence as his hands, as if he's played his whole life. His audiences sit with their mouths agape. Tears run down the audience's faces as they watch this refugee to America lift his head to the sky, as if to thank God for his blessings, all the while massaging the keys like a young genius producing the most beautiful sounds they've ever heard. His brother, Raymond? The same family story and the same exposure to music opportunities led him to be the school's drum major, leading the band in all of their performances. Access.

# Chapter 19

## THE BATTLE—DARK SIDE
## VERSUS LIGHT SIDE

The Battle by Jesse Ortiz
I am from my nana
The woman who is
Mother and Father
I am from a targeted house
Because of
The choice my uncle made
I am from the end of a gun barrel
Because of the devil's soldiers
Bury me a lost soul
Because that's the life that I live
But don't worry about me
I will give the best I can give
I am from a world of demons
But pray I will soon see God's light
And through the darkness
I will see bright white

Jesse Ortiz is in a battle, everyday. The battle is fierce and conflicted. The conflict exists between his great desire to do the right thing and be a good man, and his deep, conditioned heart to function in his reality as a soldier of the streets. He battles the two worlds of dark and light, where neither accepts the other.

To understand Jesse, one must know his background and the layers of complicated circumstances that make him who he is. Jesse was a young man raised by his nana (grandmother) because of an absent mother and a father in prison since he was a little boy. Nana was a true matriarch, as many grandmothers raising their grandchildren are. She was strong and loving, responsible and dedicated to her Jesse and his brother. As grandmothers get older and more tired, they commonly lose control of the boys that once followed their rules. She watches them become the men of the house, and these men believe they are grown and can follow their own rules. Boys living as young men who have their own rules can be dangerous and unstable.

Nana taught the boys to respect women. The streets taught them that women were just *hoes* and bitches. The messages caused conflict between Jesse's two worlds. Nana turned to the local Boys and Girls Club for help, structure, and good mentors who worked hard to help guide and lead these two young boys that Nana began to lose control of. Years of anger made it hard to forgive his father. Jesse resented the many years he had to be the one to wipe his brother's tears when he cried for their father, all the while wanting to cry himself but feeling like he had to play the strong one who had to pick up the duties of Dad. He hungered for his father, too. Even when Jesse's father got out of prison and worked so desperately to make amends with his boys, Jesse and his brother were angry and slow to trust him again.

I remember the discussion that Jesse and I had about the power of forgiveness and Jesse's initial crazy look at the thought of it. His dad didn't deserve forgiveness, as far as Jesse was concerned.

"Screw that," he said. "I'll give him the same number of years to prove he's sorry as he took away from us, and then I'll think about it."

It didn't take that long, as Jesse eventually opened up his heart to his father and their relationship began to heal as a result.

With his mother? That was a different story. Jesse saw her abandonment as even more unforgivable than his father's. At least Jesse's dad was locked up and had an excuse for not being in his life. His mom? She lived in the same community—right there, somewhere in the neighborhood. No lunch money when he needed lunch money. No new school clothes in August from his mom like most kids looked forward to. Stories of her violence and guns and drug use. According to Jesse, she spent her money on meth, not on the necessities for her children. Forgiveness wasn't in the cards for her yet. "Real eyes—Realize—Real lies," was Jesse's belief about his mom.

Besides Nana, the leaders in the Boys and Girls Club provided the best male guidance that Jesse could have had throughout his father's absence. The streets and all of its mores were also mentors to Jesse and his brother. Gangs and gangsters, his extended family living the thug life, always trying to suck Jesse in, were a constant pull toward the dark side. Jesse's uncle was MBC (Must Be Crazy, a notorious nationwide gang) and went from living with Nana at times, to living on the streets and often locked up. Being kin to MBC meant you were expected to be MBC. Depending on who was doing the coaching, what you could be and what you should be created a constantly bouncing ball for Jesse. Thus the conflict and dark side of Jesse's world.

Jesse's dark side was complex. He had core values that could cause dangerous results on the dark side. If reoriented toward good, the value from the light side would show the same magnitude of results—the embedded value of *respect* and how important that value was to Jesse. When he interpreted someone's actions as disrespecting him or anyone he loved, he reacted with actions that lead to a dark outcome. The whole street value of snitching was also embedded into Jesse's world. You handle things on your own, yourself. You don't snitch and turn to adults to handle problems. You simply take care of things yourself—by any means necessary and at any cost. Jesse's leadership in the streets made him a soldier.

The same leadership qualities from the streets were found in Jesse in his school and gave him a taste of the incredible possibilities on the light side of life as well. Jesse was a smart student with a deep insight into people. He could judge their authenticity and honesty, and if they were genuine. His communication skills were amazing; he expressed himself with the grace and confidence of a professional speaker. As a result, Jesse was often singled out for leadership opportunities where he could represent his school and community like none of the other students could.

Jesse could speak on what was right and good in people as well as he could point out the injustices of society. "Who is that kid?" was always the response from outsiders of the school who heard him speak, read his published poetry, or observed him interact with his peers and adults.

Jesse loved his school. He loved a handful of staff who had earned his respect. Earning Jesse's respect meant you were real with him. No bullshit. He could smell bullshit and insincerity from a mile away and had no tolerance of it. Jesse even questioned my authenticity at times. You couldn't be a teacher who simply said you cared about his success; he had to feel it from his heart before he opened his door to you. And when he did, he loved you to your core and never wanted to disappoint you.

There were many times he did disappoint those at school who loved him and he loved back, as the battle between dark and light was constant. Even when word of his dark actions outside of school became news to us, disappointment occurred and he felt the level of trust diminish. The deeper he participated in the dark side, the further his hope of a true light side appeared to be impossible. The battle waged one day to the next. He was drastic in his behaviors and the constant was always taking a toll on Jesse's belief system. "Who am I? Really?" is what he was conflicted by.

Understanding him is the only way to teach him. Jesse won't listen until he can be seen with clear lenses, with a willingness to see through his. The light can't be turned on until the darkness has been revealed. Three steps forward and two steps back. The temptation to give up on Jesse is always present. Then he restores faith with another step forward, a reminder of the enormous possibilities for this kid. The battle was not just his, but ours.

And his future? He says the light side feels better than the dark. I once asked him the hypothetical question of what would happen if we plucked him from this city and plopped him in another for a fresh start. Would he leave the dark side behind and go only toward the light? "Naw. I'll always be torn between both. There will always be someone tryin' to punk me out, and I just can't have that, Ms. Riggs."

> 1,000 Miles by Jesse Ortiz
> Look into my eyes and judge me if you want
> I don't care
> Because to find someone willing to walk in your shoes
> Is rare
> If I don't write how I feel
> The closet would be closed
> And the sadness behind this clown mask
> Wouldn't be exposed
> To walk in my shoes would be like feeling
> Death on your back
> And you fight everyday to make sure your
> Life line don't go flat
> Every day the reaper puts me on trial
> So before you judge me
> Put on my shoes
> And walk 1,000 miles

So before we judge him, before we play the reaper, we walk in his shoes. His shoes are big. They are sturdy, weathering the storms and the fights and the pull of his two worlds. One, the world he can't seem to get away from, and the other he dabbles in, tasting the sweetness of success and attention that puts him in the limelight of greatness. His shoes show experience and range, with parts of them dirty with blood and sweat and parts exposing remnants of shine and polish. His shoes feel rough like his outside. His shoes feel soft like his heart. Before we judge him, we walk in his shoes. And we hold on to *hope*, worrying about the dark side and believing in the light, as he walks across the stage and receives his diploma, one last glance as his red cap and gown step off the stairs of the stage and into the bigger world, on his own. Wear those shoes, Jesse. Show this world what you can be. Jesse is a love story.

Note: Jesse Ortiz is really Jesse Ortiz. No name change to protect his truth. "I want people to know my truth, Ms. Riggs. Don't change my name."

# Chapter 20

## CARLOS AND DANA,
## A FATAL ATTRACTION

Two minutes left on the clock. It's overtime. The crowd inside the gym goes crazy as the score ties between the two rival schools. The sound of the referee's whistle blows for a timeout. The band plays another song and the cheerleaders chant as both teams put their heads together for another play to get the game won.

I reluctantly exit the gym to get ready to supervise the hallway that will soon be packed with exiting fans. It takes me just a second, but I realize, in the midst of the wild excitement of the game, I'm the lone adult in the corridor outside the gym and just up ahead, a battle is about to begin.

My body goes tense with the anticipation of the ugliness that I see is about to unfold. I glance around to see if there is any help. I jog toward the trouble. Just me. No security, no staff, no police around to assist. I grab desperately for the radio at my waist to get somebody else out there with me, wondering where everyone is as the radio drops to the floor. I pick it up, breathless, and call for assistance in the hallway.

"I'm about . . . to have a problem . . . outside the gym," I say, huffing and puffing as I pick up speed. But no one can hear me because of all the noise. No time to go get anyone. I'm angry because I realize they must all be watching the game.

Devante, from the Southside Family Blood's gang is posted up in his own uniform of orange shirt and khaki pants, leaning against the massive windows where he's held his spot of power throughout most of the game. That's where Southside Family always stands after the game. His posture is firm and his body faces forward like he owns the spot, but his head is tilted down as he has a conversation with his regular coolness, not to his boys, but to Dana.

Their conversation is soft; it's private and flirty and anyone watching could tell what was happening. I know right away that it means trouble. Dana's not Devante's girl. She belongs to Carlos, and Carlos is here somewhere. No dude gets to talk to Dana and everybody knows that. Devante knows that, too.

All of a sudden Carlos comes around the corner and is just ten steps in front of me picking up speed to get to Devante. He probably got a text from someone snitching on Dana.

"Man, your girl's out in the hallway with Southside."

Carlos, in a rage says, "What the fuck, man, what you tryin' to rap to my girl, motha fucker?"

He's aggressive and loud and Dana knows the trouble is about to go down. She's seen that fire in Carlos's eyes, many times. Devante remains cool with a grin that mocks Carlos's insecurity about his girl. Devante's calm makes Carlos even angrier.

"Nigga, man, you betta check your girl, not me, homeboy," says Devante with eyes full of a stare and an expression that means he's got *no* fear of Carlos or his rant.

Dana and I rush between them, holding Carlos back and trying to pull him away. Devante remains perched like an eagle protecting his nest, not about to look as if the problem is his.

"Let's go, Carlos. Out this door. Now," I say with the same force I've put into my arms to move him away. He moves with me, fighting me the whole time and constant with more words for Devante.

"Bitch, I'll fuck you up if you touch my girl."

Dana begs Carlos to stop, desperate for him to see she's his property, not Devante's. She pushes her arm out at me to let her handle the situation.

"Just stop and leave us alone," she says to me as the three of us move through the door outside the school. "I can handle Carlos; just let me talk to him," she demands, more firmly to me this time, as if I'm going to let her be in charge of the situation and leave her to take over from here.

"No, Dana. I'm not going to just let you handle this. I need him out of here."

She goes wild with insistence and is now as out of control as Carlos. "Just get your ass back inside the school, bitch. I got this!" Dana screamed, her arm waving and her finger pointed from my face to the direction of the building. She didn't care. She was so into taking care of her man and her world with him that she wouldn't remember she even called her principal a bitch. It was all about showing off to Carlos and cleaning up the mess she'd started. It was that, "Please, baby, it isn't what it looks like" clean up that she was in a hurry to resolve with her man, her hands cupped around Carlos's face, desperately trying to get him to look at her while he had his eyes plastered on Devante through the windows.

I could see it wasn't close to being over. "Where is everyone?" I wanted to scream, as Carlos suddenly tried to take a run for the door on the other side of Devante, ready to rush up on him and cold cock him. I yanked at his shirt and somehow found enough strength to stop him from getting to the door, all while Dana ran after him, too, focused on him instead of me.

Finally, there was a flurry of security and police that pushed through the doors and showed up to help, probably only taking a few minutes from the time the conflict began, but having felt like an hour until they did. Two of them took Dana and Carlos and guided them off campus. I went back in the school to find Devante, the same cool calm he had when I left. He was almost too calm, like Southside Family always appeared to be in school—that calm that means, "We won't handle this here. We'll take care of this outside of school."

140

I knew that if Devante wanted to handle Carlos, it wouldn't be in school. It would no doubt be handled in the streets the way Southside Family always handled their business. Soon his boys would know. And soon, if Devante wanted it, Carlos would get jumped for rushin' at Devante that way, frontin' him in public.

I stood with security and one of the police officers after the incident and let them know I never wanted to have that hallway unsupervised, no matter how good the game was or how much someone wanted to step away to get popcorn. My heart was still beating fast and my voice showed of anger.

"There are enough of us around that *all* of these areas should be covered. I was in this one alone, fellas," I said.

"Here, Ms. Riggs, you need to take this and keep it on you. These kids are dangerous and you need to be able to protect yourself," said one of the officers.

My quizzical eyes moved from looking at his very serious face to looking down at his hands. I was surprised to see him handing me a can of mace.

"Mace? Oh, my God, no. I would *never* use that on my kids."

He glared at me, disappointed that I wouldn't even consider his method of control. We looked at each other with the same intensity as if to say to each other, "Are you nuts?" Me, because I meant it. I couldn't imagine reaching for something that would harm any of my kids, no matter what was happening. Him, because he meant it, too. He wouldn't hesitate for a second to use it on those same kids—the ones he sees as dangerous. Maybe it was better that he wasn't there when the mess went down. This incident was over. It was done. No mace. No one hurt.

The fatal attraction continued. Carlos and Dana would continue to be that couple that everyone talked about at school. The kids, the adults, would all say, "Those two are going to kill each other someday," a prophecy I prayed would never be true, but worried in my heart that it could be a reality. They could be the couple we'd read about in the paper someday: that same old story of the domestic violence situation that started in a fight and led to a murder, maybe even murder-suicide. The story will be the same, only the names will be different and this time we'll recognize them—awful visuals and ones I didn't hesitate to describe to Carlos and Dana, every time they had another incident that sounded like a movie. They were that couple that couldn't be together because they fought all the time. That same couple that couldn't be apart because they couldn't handle the thought of each other with someone else. Make up, to break up. Fight hard. Love hard. The cycle continues.

There were multiple volatile situations followed by makeup sessions with plenty of new promises. Situations, too many times, occurred at school and led to a hallway or cafeteria scene. They once had a cafeteria confrontation that led to a carton of milk being thrown by one at the other, an ugly scene in front of all their classmates; just one more picture in the minds of their friends who may one day say, "I'm not surprised. You should have seen them in high school." There were meetings with both kids and both parents, multiple times, always with promises of counseling to address their need to control their anger with each other. Even if they parted from each other, they would each pick someone similar the next time around.

They started counseling only because we insisted on it for them to remain at school, but they ended it too soon for any lessons to be learned. Both understood their issues were dangerous, but they were screamers who didn't listen to each other, shouting over each other and blaming the other for their problems. Dana's dad was worried about his daughter's future with the makeup of this relationship and would often criticize her for how she acted. She always jumped to remind him where she learned it. Neither Dana nor Carlos would acknowledge their own issues. Both would say the right things to be able to get back into school, agreeing to our guidelines, and following them, only for a while.

Another incident involving the two would lead to Carlos being removed from the soccer team, the thing he loved the most, but not enough to stay away from Dana. And still another would almost take him out of a leadership opportunity that was given to him in hopes of trying to get him to see his potential.

Eventually, the two were separated at school, as much as we could separate them, rearranging their schedules so that one attended in the morning and the other in the afternoon. Still, this young pair, desperate to be together and refusing to be apart no matter what anyone else insisted, were always side-by-side outside of school. Both were on track to graduate and both were college bound with good grades and promising futures ahead of them. Their individual potential was why we kept trying to hang on to them when we probably should have separated them into different schools long before the end. We felt their being together would eventually lead to their demise.

The last straw occurred at an end-of-the-year event. The incident was disruptive enough to force us to not allow them to walk across the stage with their classmates. We could no longer hold our breath and cross our fingers, hoping they'd behave as they promised. These two, instead, received their diplomas in the mail. No pomp. No circumstance. No memories. Having to celebrate privately on their own, who knows how.

Both students ultimately went on to college. They remained a couple as college started, hopefully growing to be healthier as individuals, there to support each other, and learning how to disagree respectfully. If not, going on their own way to stay safe and be happy.

# Chapter 21

## *THOSE* KIDS

Ask for help and great teachers swarm to step up and take care of their own. Example after example abound, heartwarming stories where dedicated teachers will go to any means necessary to help those kids.

For instance, the teacher who shows up at school with a brand new bike for the student whose only mode of transportation to school, her bike, was stolen. "Don't tell her who it's from. Just make sure she gets it, Ms. Riggs," she said, humble about the gift.

The same teacher made sure she received gift cards to a grocery store for food that her family refused to provide for her because she was "eighteen and should be feeding herself."

Another teacher took her personal day to show up in court, advocating for a young man at risk of going to jail for a theft charge—all because she believed in her student and what a second chance would do for him if a judge would just listen to her plea.

A coach, season after season, and all through the off-season, fills his van full of players that need a ride home after practice and games. The same coach dips into his own pocket to purchase new basketball shoes for the player that can't afford them, just so the young man won't be teased about the condition of his old ones.

The teacher of a homeless boy, who had no one to represent him at an awards banquet, insisted on being his guest and the one who loved him enough to sit beside him at the table, honoring his efforts and showing her belief in his future.

A counselor used her access with a friend, a mechanic, enabled her student's car to get fixed. The student, who felt defeated and hopeless, unable to get to her job for work, unable to transport her baby to daycare and also attend school was rejuvenated and restored of her faith in her future.

A counselor wrote a grant to purchase bus tickets for all of the students who needed transportation to our Saturday Credit Recovery Program. "No excuses. Get here and we'll help you get back on track to graduate."

The same young counselor gets on the phone and calls kids when they are late for Saturday school.

Many teachers emptied their closets, kitchens, garages, and storage to set a student's family up for the home they would finally move into after leaving a shelter they'd stayed in for months: from homelessness to a home because of teachers.

Many teachers constantly seek out new strategies and any professional development opportunity that will assist *them* in teaching differently so their students will be successful.

Who are these teachers? They are people who teach with their hearts instead of textbooks. They are educators who have it. That "it factor" that oozes a natural belief that all kids, no matter who they are, what they look like, what mistakes they make, what their backgrounds are, or what baggage they bring through our doors, are valuable and capable. The kids know who they are. The word gets out. They beg to get them as their teacher for another year, just to be assured they'll be loved in their next level of academic endeavor. For emotional safety, those requests are their insurance for the encouragement they've already experienced.

"I know I'll be okay with her." Those teachers are the ones students come back to visit. Those are the teachers students invite to their college graduations and weddings, and are first informed about the births of their children.

The power of a caring and dedicated teacher is life changing to kids that others have given up on. The power of a school filled with staff that is ample in heart is truly phenomenal and can change the lives of those kids, forever.

Just as powerful is the teacher without heart—powerfully damaging—who constantly complains and makes judgmental comments that scar kids for life. They sprinkle poison in the atmosphere of the departmental office space and teachers' lounge. They speak poorly of those kids from their school when they sit in the beauty shop or at their dinner parties, sharing only the dirty business of the family so that strangers then tell their own versions of what they heard from a teacher, like the natural effects of telephone gossip.

"You know what I heard happened at such-and-such school? If a teacher told me that happened, it must be true of all of those kids. I'd never send my kid to that school with those kids."

The heartless teachers try to sabotage any efforts for positive school change that requires hard work, hoping to recruit colleagues who will jump on their own bandwagons of mediocrity or less, all with the purpose of making themselves feel better about their own laziness and refusal to change.

"Those kids can't do this level of work. They just can't learn this stuff."

"Those kids can't go to college, so I don't know why we tell them they can."

Those kinds of teachers have a high rate of failure, and their excuses of why are plentiful.

"I'm not calling home to parents because half of their phones are disconnected and most of them don't even speak English."

Professional development? "I don't have time" as if there is nothing new they can learn or need to learn. They are the ones who can be seen sprinting to their cars early and never showing up for anything beyond their contractual obligations, and are the first to call their union reps and report a principal who is forcing them to do more.

The late rapper Biggie Smalls, a.k.a. The Notorious B.I.G. in his hip hop hit, "Juicy," raps,

"Yeah, this album is dedicated to all the teachers that told me I'd never amount to nothin'... Uh-ha. It's all good. And if you don't know, now you know, nigga, uh-ha."

Sweet revenge for the young man who took his skills to the top of the charts; his music still played in MP3 players around the world long after his early, violent death. What kind of teacher, counselor, administrator, cafeteria lady, security guard, or anyone who works in a school, tells a kid they'll never amount to anything? For a kid to run into one is too many.

Multiple exposures to these kinds of heartless teachers can take a happy, motivated, and hopeful kid and diminish their fragile hearts to believing that stuff that B.I.G. rapped about. Ask a dropout why he left school. Many of them reference, "I hated school," or "I didn't think anyone cared." Kids who have nothing but this kind of story to tell about their school experience translate to, "We've failed our kids," and diminish all of the stories that aren't being told.

My most sincere hope and the motive behind writing this book is that the real stories about our kids can be told and society will listen hard. And that our society will gain a better understanding of the dedicated people in urban schools, saving souls every day, and that they far outnumber those who somehow call themselves educators, but really are not.

In our school, without a doubt, I believe the individual success comes from those majority of passionate and dedicated teachers who so obviously love *our* students. Even when they don't love everything they do, they hang in there with them and remain the resilient adults who those kids need, not giving up on them. They focus on their strengths and their potential. They know they are not successful until their kids are. These teachers far outweigh the ineffective and are who I give all credit to our school's increased enrollment.

This book was written to help all of society begin to care about all of our kids, not just some of society about some of the kids. Our government, at both the state and federal levels, will continue to push accountability, as it should, but should understand that we cannot judge a student's achievement solely on the measurement of a test score, and should, instead, assess schools and teachers and students on their improvement and growth.

If I would have been ultimately judged on my test scores alone throughout my academic years as a young student, I would have given up and been seen as a failure under today's state and federal guidelines. My experience in the urban schools with those kids has convinced me that our country is filled with great *hope* for a future full of this generation of young people contributing to our world with great creativity, gusto, and heart. Their stories are my love stories. And I'm honored to share them.

# IF THEY ONLY KNEW YOU

Written and performed as a gift to the students of Omaha South High School, at a poetry slam, by their principal.

If they only knew you, they'd know you.

We see beautiful faces, brown and black, white and red...

Hair, so silky and shiny ... braided and aftro'd ... locks of dread and locks of curls ... purple and blue ... You and You and You.

They judge you on your surface ... by your skin tone, the style of your clothes ... how low you wear your pants and how visible are those tattoos ... the neighborhood from which your bus travels, and if you claim a set ... or whether you have a social ... As if these things define you? How simple is their judgment ... how cheated are they *not* to look with depth.

If they only knew you, they'd know you.

If they only knew you, they'd know you and they wouldn't be so harsh.

How dare they have no faith in you and believe you won't climb high ... when they don't know your stories ... You see, it's your real stories of perseverance, survival and stick-to-it-iv-ness that paint the portraits of who you are.

Those portraits reveal that you have dreams, too.

Intricate strokes that paint the truths that you reach for anything that spells *hope* ... H-O-P-E.

That you want that American Dream of *success* ... S-U-C-C-E-S-S and that spells M-O-N-E-Y.

If they only knew you, they'd know you.

If they only knew you, they'd know you and they would know you strive for college. Campus and sorority and majors and degrees and that second graduation that shouts, "I've made it ... look out world, I'm here."

If they only knew you, they'd know you and they'd march to form a crowd ... a mob to feel your energy and clamber to lift their arms and their voices to rejoice in your greatness ... they'd say, "Who ... are ... these ... genius minds that fill these halls?" Genius minds with huge hearts ... with courageous souls. If they only knew you, they'd know you ... You *are* South High.

# ACKNOWLEDGEMENTS

The love stories in this book come with many thanks to people in my life who have supported me throughout my career, and certainly through the process of putting these stories down on paper. Without them, this project would not have been finished and I acknowledge each of them with the sincerest gratitude.

My mother, Madeline Churchich, played an amazing role as Mom and showed me the gift of love and kindness, always preaching, "The more you give, the more you get back." That certainly has been my reward for a long career in education. I have been given back so much.

My late father, Ely Churchich, always showed me the power of a Daddy to a little girl. You made me feel like I was five, all the way up to your death. I have walked down the halls of my school and understood that so many of our girls would give anything to have just one day with a Daddy like you, whom I was blessed to have for forty-two years. Thank you for all the times I called you from school after a really hard day and begged you to find a spot in your business for me. You always said, "Don't be silly! You are doing exactly what you were meant to do. Come over and have a glass of wine, and it will be all right tomorrow." You were correct. Tomorrow was always better. I miss you, my sweet Daddy.

My brother, Jeff Churchich, and my sister, Suzanne Mariucci, who always told me how proud they were of me. Your own successes have been so great, yet you always made me feel valued in our family. I have been blessed to have such a beautiful family.

My BFF, Patti Quinn-McGovern, the best cheerleader a girl could have. Thank you for never making me feel like the demands of my career did anything to diminish the beauty, strength, and consistency of our friendship. You are my brightest sunshine.

My superintendent, Dr. John Mackiel, is such an incredible leader and personal supporter of my career. You told me it was me who needed to tell the stories and reveal the truth about the depth of challenges our students face. "It has to be you who tells the story, Cara." I'll never forget how you have believed in me and my work. My loyalty to you is never ending.

My rock in education, Luanne Nelson. Thank you for being my friend, confidant, and savior during every challenge I faced as a principal. You gave me courage during times I did not know I had it. "Are you having a good hair day?" will forever be ingrained in my memory, as your preface to all of the times you made me face the media!

To my girls, the TAHs: Thank you for the years of sharing the highs, the lows, the sad, and the hilarious of our world as teachers. Thank you for your inspiration and sisterhood. Our careers brought us together, but our hearts are the glue that will forever keep us bonded. Thanks, too, for making me believe I could really tell these love stories so others could benefit from their lessons. Our road trips to the lake house have created over a decade of validation of the power of female friendship.

My friend, Wes Hall, an author, motivational speaker, and teacher trainer who gave me the inspiration to get this book written. You convinced me I was a good storyteller and that I needed to stop talking about doing it and, "Get it did!" (Smile) "Some stories have to be written," you always told me, "and some stories are being written for you. If it is not in *your* voice, rewrite it." These words kept me focused throughout the writing process. Thank you for your encouragement to persevere and for convincing me that my pen could be powerful and *my* voice significant.

Bishop William Barlowe, my friend and personal advisor for decades on issues of love and life, and in times of crisis. You helped me stay focused on "What I want to be when I grow up." This book is something you have encouraged me to do for years. (Can we co-author the next one?) Thank you for always reminding me that God has driven my professional destiny. You are saving souls, everyday. Your church has been a hospital for sinners to many of the gang members and other students lost in the paralysis of believing there was no way out. Thank you for the many times we have teamed up to show students throughout the years that their situations can change.

Alberto Gonzales shared my vision. Thank you for all of your support, no matter which school I have been in. I see you as the "Mayor of South Omaha" and I appreciate how you welcomed me into your community and made me feel a part of the family. There's no place like home in South Omaha! You are an amazing man and a great friend.

To the many talented teachers and administrative teams who have given me confidence in the public schools. It is evident to me that most educators are talented, are in the profession for the right reasons, and take the education of all of our students seriously. We know, as a dedicated family, who the untalented and nonpassionate colleagues are. Thank you for making it obvious to me who the very best of you are as individuals. If you are not on that list, I hope you know who you are and that you reconsider your career path. It is not too late, and it is too important that you move over and make room for those who want to make a difference and who are great at it. If you are not passionate, inspiring, and getting students to learn in your classroom, you are likely damaging them. The power of a teacher, both positively and negatively, is so great.

CPSIA information can be obtained at www.ICGtesting.com
Printed in the USA
LVOW130103160513

333859LV00004B/5/P